ROBERT LOUIS STEVENSON (1

Robert Louis Balfour Stevenson wa
essayist and travel writer. His most
Island, *Kidnapped* and *The Strange*
Hyde.

NEIL BARTLETT

Neil Bartlett's adaptations and translations have been performed
by the National, the Royal Shakespeare Company, the Glasgow
Citizens and the Abbey in Dublin – as well as by theatres,
schools and colleges around the world. They include new
realisations of Albert Camus' *The Plague*, Dumas' *Camille*,
Charles Dickens' *Oliver Twist*, *A Christmas Carol* and *Great
Expectations*, Genet's *Splendid's* and *The Maids*, Kleist's *The
Prince of Homburg*, Labiche's *The Threesome*, Marivaux's *The
Dispute*, *The Island of Slaves* and *The Game of Love and
Chance*, Molière's *The School for Wives*, *The Misanthrope* and
Don Juan, Racine's *Berenice* and Oscar Wilde's *The Picture of
Dorian Gray*.

His plays include *A Vision of Love Revealed in Sleep* (Traverse
and Drill Hall), *Sarrasine* (Lyric Hammersmith), *Night After
Night* (Royal Court), *Stella* (LIFT), *In Extremis* and *Or You
Could Kiss Me* (both commissioned by and performed at the
National Theatre, London). As a theatre director and
performance-maker he has created work for Artangel, Tate
Britain, the Manchester Royal Exchange, the Bristol Old Vic,
the Manchester International Festival, the Edinburgh
International Festival, the Aldeburgh Festival, the Brighton
Festival, the Holland Festival – and for spaces as diverse as
Southwark Cathedral and the Royal Vauxhall Tavern.

From 1994 to 2005 he was Artistic Director of the Lyric Theatre
Hammersmith, and in 2000 he was awarded an OBE for his
work there. Neil is also a novelist; his titles as an author include
Ready to Catch Him Should he Fall (1990), *Mr Clive and Mr
Page* (1996), *Skin Lane* (2007), *The Disappearance Boy* (2014)
and *Address Book* (2021). You can find out more about Neil's
work, and contact him, at www.neil-bartlett.com

Other Titles in This Series

Robert Louis Stevenson

JEKYLL AND HYDE

adapted for the stage by
Neil Bartlett

NICK HERN BOOKS
London
www.nickhernbooks.co.uk

A Nick Hern Book

This adaptation of *Jekyll and Hyde* first published in Great Britain as a paperback original in 2022 by Nick Hern Books Limited, The Glasshouse, 49a Goldhawk Road, London W12 8QP

Jekyll and Hyde copyright © 2022 Neil Bartlett
Introduction copyright © 2022 Neil Bartlett

Lyrics of 'When I Survey the Wondrous Cross' by Isaac Watts (1707); 'Maybe It's Because I'm a Londoner' Words and Music by Hubert Gregg © 1947. Reproduced by permission of Francis Day and Hunter Ltd/Sony Music Publishing, London W1T 3LP

Cover image: Nicholas Shaw in the original production; photo by Grant Archer

Designed and typeset by Nick Hern Books, London
Printed in the UK by Mimeo Ltd, Huntingdon, Cambridgeshire PE29 6XX

A CIP catalogue record for this book is available from the British Library

ISBN 978 1 83904 123 5

Woodland
CARBON
www.woodlandcarbon.co.uk
NICK HERN BOOKS
Printed on Carbon Captured paper

Contents

Introduction
Neil Bartlett

A Synopsis of the Story

It is 1886. A female doctor opens the show by recalling that when
she was a newly qualified member of staff in a London hospital
she found herself presented with a horrendous case of assault on a
teenage girl. In trying to establish the identity of the girl's
assailant, this pioneering doctor found herself drawn into a dark
story of male violence and privilege. Undeterred, she tracked the
culprit down – and found him lurking right in the heart of the
same conservative male Establishment which ran the hospital
where she had just started working. By confronting this horror – a
horror made darker by the fact that the assailant turned out to be a
doctor himself, with all sorts of personal and professional
glamour attached to his name – she finally found the nerve
required to fully commit herself to her chosen profession.

The Telling of the Story

The synopsis above may surprise you if you were expecting a
'straight' adaptation of this world-famous Gothic masterpiece.
After all, one of the most disturbing things about Robert Louis
Stevenson's original novel is that it is set in an all-male world;
there are no female characters at all apart from one speechless
child and a couple of barely glimpsed servants. The terrifying
experiments to which Sigmund Freud's contemporary, Dr
Jekyll, subjects his own privileged, masculine body are some of
the nineteenth century's great explorations of identity; however,
while I very much wanted to keep those experiments within a
dark and all-male world – to exploit to the full, in other words,
the dramatic potential of the creepy gentleman's club-plus-
drugs-and-sex feeling of the original novel – I also wanted to
throw that world into relief by way of a questioning and
resilient female perspective.

I've tried to do this first of all by simply making the female characters of the original both real and crucial. The girl who gets assaulted at the very start of the story has become an actual person as opposed to a cipher (albeit a masterfully haunting one; I think the page describing Mr Hyde's initial attack on her is one of the most unnerving pieces of prose of Stevenson's entire career). Dr Jekyll's barely there housemaid, meanwhile, has been promoted to being his housekeeper, and also – as my work on adapting the story has developed – morphed into a hospital matron who now not only takes charge of some very significant sections of the story but also of the space within which that story is told.

Secondly, I have invented a whole new character, Dr Stevenson. Her journey from furious revulsion to appalled fascination with the man who is eventually proved to have assaulted her patient may seem like pure invention on my part; in fact, my use of this invented character as a kind of forensic detective very closely follows the way in which Stevenson himself uses a Russian-doll, story-within-story structure for his novel. The effect of this is to take us inexorably closer to the divided life of his terrifying (anti-)hero – and finally, right inside Jekyll's diseased and divided mind. And for those of you who doubt that there could *actually* be a female doctor in a London hospital at the end of the nineteenth century, I would point you to the strange case of the woman who won the gold medal for surgery at the medical school attached to the Royal Free Hospital in London in 1899. Her name? Dr Mabel Geraldine *Stevenson*. It was seeing this real Dr Stevenson's name still proudly displayed up on a memorial in one of the hospital's more out-of-the-way corridors that first triggered the whole idea of this character.

The other big change I've made in my theatrical retelling of the story is that I've given it a chorus. The male characters in the story not only play their own individual parts, they also act as a single if multi-headed entity. Sometimes, they act en masse in order to both embody and amplify Jekyll's upper-class masculine entitlement; as he changes into his alter-ego Hyde, they warp and distort with him, becoming an ensemble physicalisation of the gibbering, ape-like energies which are the dark mirror of that entitlement. Again, this apparently bold idea

was inspired by the original novel. One of the reasons why this
story has never gone out of print, I think – and why people who
have never read it or even heard of its author are familiar with
its title – is that Stevenson somehow makes us believe that his
Dr Jekyll is not merely some random, split-personality
psychopath, but that his parallel existence as Mr Hyde tells us
something profoundly true about how masculinity functions in
our society. In other words, about how we continue to both
forbid and permit male bodies to dream of doing their worst.

This idea of all the men in the company working as a chorus
also foregrounds the fact that this script was very much written
for an ensemble. It requires the actors to deploy lots of
physicality, and to take a pitch-black and sometimes ghoulishly
comic delight in switching between roles and moods. For
everyone in the company, at key moments, there is a direct
storytelling connection with the audience; for everyone, there is
cut-and-thrust dialogue taken directly from Stevenson's restless
and haunted original. In the great final sequence of the story,
when we see Jekyll and Hyde fight to the death for possession
of the doctor's soul, it is the supporting energy of this chorus
that gives (I hope) this fatal struggle its necessary scale and
impact.

The Setting

Although individual scenes in the story have specific locations,
this adaptation presumes that the story is told swiftly,
inventively, within a single setting and without any pauses for
blacked-out scene changes. Sound and light can be as Gothic, or
not, as budget, taste and playing space dictate. I have, after all,
seen other scripts of mine done with the full resources of a
major London theatre, and then by a handful of actors in a bare
upstairs room of a pub. In the end (and the beginning), the only
thing that matters in this kind of theatre is the telling of the
story.

That said, the implied environment of the script does seem to be
medical in some way – perhaps an anatomy theatre or morgue
or ward. Whatever decisions any future productions of it take, I

x JEKYLL AND HYDE

think it's important that the chorus of men can be in some way above and behind the women when they are not in a scene. While I was writing, I found an extraordinary picture of pioneering doctor Elizabeth Garrett Anderson being examined by a Board of Faculty in Paris (it's on her Wikipedia page, if you want to look it up). It was this picture that inspired the script's opening image of a bunch of black-suited Victorian gentlemen – a hospital board – looking down on a woman. They are the patriarchy, literally judging an upstart female.

You'll notice that in the script people often interject that phrase 'Thank you!' in order to interrupt, initiate or curtail something. As often as not, this is a call to some implied technician or flyman for a lighting or sound cue. In other words, the characters are often both in the scene and in a theatre.

The Timing

For all that it is so powerfully interior – as much an investigation of the mind, as well as of the body – *The Strange Case of Dr Jekyll and Mr Hyde* is also first and foremost a thriller. I would therefore recommend that the first half should have a pacey running time of just over an hour, and the second half of a good bit under. As the for operation of time in the story itself – i.e. of the gaps between Mr Hyde's various crimes – I have condensed the events of the original novel quite a bit. For those of you who want to compare my sequence of events with Stevenson's original, I've included a timeline as an appendix after the script itself (pp. 96–97).

The Singing

From the idea of having a chorus who whisper, gibber, groan and sometimes speak in full choric unison, it was a short leap to the idea that they might sometimes sing. To that end, I've given Mr Hyde a music-hall song as a theme tune – 'Maybe It's Because I'm a Londoner' by Hubert Gregg – to be whistled or muttered or quoted by his supporters as his *leitmotif*. I've also suggested underscoring certain sequences with the gentlemen of the chorus singing a particularly bloodthirsty hymn. After all,

Stevenson never fully left behind either the imagery or the scars of his Christian upbringing, and they underwrite every detail of this story of his in particular.

As for the rest of the sound-world, my playlist while writing included a lot of Siouxsie Sioux and a fair bit of Bauhaus. British Goth music – and some of its early influences, especially in the world of radical electronica – seems to me a good contemporary match for Stevenson's imagination. It also helped remind me that he was writing a dark, dodgy and highly experimental work of modern popular fiction, not a literary 'classic'.

The Tricks and Transformations

An audience comes to this story expecting transformations. So, how are they to be done?

Again, I am happy to leave all answers to that question to future actors and directors – but as you'll see, the script does contain some built-in suggestions.

Basically, the changes are all done with, through or behind or a door. In the story, the two symbolically contrasting doors of Jekyll's London house are so strongly evoked that they are almost characters. One is shabby, stained and 'queer'; this is the back door which is used exclusively by Mr Hyde. The other is shiny, respectable – as befits its being in a *very* expensive neighbourhood – and is used only by Dr Jekyll and his society dinner guests. The trick, of course, is that they both give access to the same address (this is a feature, by the way, that Stevenson borrowed from his own boyhood home in Edinburgh). I've simply suggested that the two doors should be literally back to back – that one be the reverse of the other.

Also in my mind while writing this adaptation has been the idea of a magician's cabinet – one of those big boxes with doors that get wheeled on, spun round to show you there's nothing round the back or inside – from which people can be made to appear, disappear, and even transform. For this image, I was inspired by the famous quote from Stevenson where he describes how the story first came to him in a nightmare: 'All I first dreamed about

Dr Jekyll' – he says – 'was that a man was being pressed into a cabinet, when he swallowed a drug and changed into another being…'

The trickery involved in doing the transformations in the way I suggest is actually quite simple: all that is required is the use of doubling and a spot of misdirection – while one of the company slips offstage – and a clear use of costume changes. But it should add a lot of tension – and pleasure – to the staging.

Eventually, of course, the audience must be tricked into believing that they see Jekyll turn into Hyde before their very eyes. For that (as you'll see) I suggest using the chorus. In other words, to have *them* embody and multiply Dr Jekyll's famous two-bodied-ness. This should give plenty of sinister spectacle – and also communicate this story's most fundamental idea, namely the one that 'doubleness' might be lurking inside anyone's body. To this end, the physical work of the ensemble will be crucial to the playing of the script – and to making the audience believe that they really see Jekyll turn into Hyde and back again, without any cinematic trickery involved.

The Characters

These notes are based on the assumption that the script is played by an ensemble of nine. Of course, it could be played by more than nine actors – and I'd love to see someone do it with fewer.

Dr Stevenson

Stevenson is a newly qualified doctor, recently admitted to a previously all-male profession. She's (fairly) young, and tough – but it is also really important that she's inexperienced. Every man she meets is her superior, and every doctor she meets could get her sacked. At key moments, she is dangerously attracted to the glamorous and controversial Dr Jekyll. She is intimidated by him – and also finally pushed beyond her fears into anger and action.

The Girl

Mr Hyde's first victim in the novel is a young (seven or eight years old) working-class girl who appears on page three... and then promptly disappears on the same page. Shockingly – and brilliantly, from the point of view of accurately portraying male violence – Stevenson's original narrative treats this girl exactly as Hyde treats her: as an accident with no consequences. As you'll see, I've given her a voice, and made the violence against her the real starting point of the story. Finding out who assaulted this girl – and by implication wanting to identify the culprit in order to prevent further attacks – is really what drives Dr Stevenson and the Matron (see below) on in their search for the truth.

In this version of the story, the girl is slightly older. Picking up on the weird salaciousness of the way Hyde assaults her in the original, I have made her an underage (by our standards) casual sex-worker. She is (of course, given her class and era) illiterate – and fearless. Importantly, a street girl like her would never have been in a hospital before. In the script, as you will see, this character has remained nameless. This is not an oversight, but has been done so that any actor who plays her can christen the character themselves, once they have got to know her during rehearsals.

The Hospital Matron

The Matron works in the hospital where Dr Stevenson has just been posted – but is much more experienced. In a practical sense, she runs the ward, and therefore the stage. She would definitely never have worked with a female doctor before – perhaps she needs to be convinced a woman can do it? Professionally, she is as solid as a rock; stern, efficient and robust. The Matron doubles as Mrs Poole in the story. In this embodiment, she shows borderline-unpleasant relish for its bloodiest moment of physical horror. She also needs christening.

So, three strong and remarkable women; now, the six men in the company. I would say that it's important to notice how each of these men already has a 'Hyde' side to their character. None of them is squeaky-clean. If you pay close attention to the story, you will notice that the reason these men fail to catch the criminal in their midst is because they are either consciously or unconsciously on his side.

Mr Enfield

A pompous, middle-aged 'man about town' – but with a few dodgy habits beneath his bluster. For instance, what exactly *was* he doing on the street where he first meets Mr Hyde, at 3 a.m.?

Mr Utterson

A very senior and well-connected lawyer. He was at school and college with Jekyll, and is now his solicitor. He presents himself as leading a life (as he sees it) of iron-willed self-control and propriety. But he lies, often – or at least prevaricates – and deliberately withholds information both from the police and the audience. Crucially, he refuses to believe anything truly dodgy about his old school friend until it is way too late. Offered the chance by the narrative to finally do the right thing, he stays loyal to his class and his gender, and refuses to humiliate himself by publicly admitting that he's done anything wrong.

Dr Lanyon

An older, conservative doctor. He was also at school with Jekyll, but I reckon a few years above him, as he presents as distinctively old-school. He too suspects the worst – and again, does nothing about it until it's too late. His refusal to kill Hyde when he has the chance is, I think, paradoxically admirable.

Inspector Newcome

Newcome's work as a detective is crucially hampered by the simple fact that he completely fails to imagine that the criminal might be from the same class as his informants, and so just assumes that he is looking for a random psychopath.

Mr Guest

A clerk in Dr Utterson's legal chambers. He seems to love the gruesomeness of murder and crime – and completely fails to see anything dodgy in that fascination, or in the innuendo-laden 'banter' he makes of it.

Collectively, these five actors are referred to in the script as 'The Gentlemen'. When required to do so, they also chip in and play any minor parts that the story needs to be filled at notice. And – please note – one of them at least should be physically similar enough in height, build and silhouette to the actor playing Dr Jekyll to double for him in the substitution trick just before (spoiler alert) the death of Mr Hyde at the end of Act One. The script *doesn't* attribute particular lines to particular actors when they are speaking as a chorus – the parts of the script that are printed in bold. All that will have to be worked out in rehearsals. The use of bold does *not* indicate that all the Gentlemen speak all of their lines all the time. Indeed, the trick of them all speaking in unison should probably be used very sparingly.

Sitting in the middle of these five men at the top of the show is a male figure who is apparently the leader of this slice of the Establishment. This, in fact, is:

Dr Jekyll

In Stevenson's original novel, Jekyll is fifty – but for us he could easily be thirty-five or forty. In other words, he is in his prime: respected, cultivated, *extremely* wealthy – and single. When he is wearing evening dress (in which I would recommend that he looks suavely and even dangerously handsome), he seems almost like a character out of the works of his contemporary Oscar Wilde; he has a Wildean command of language, and also that characteristic Wildean combination of silky-smooth intellectual superiority with profound guilt and secrecy. The most important thing of all about him is, of course, that he is a top-ranking doctor; in contemporary terms, he should be thought of as a senior consultant. When he was

young, he drank and used sex-workers – just like any other
gentleman of his class – but now his hobby is working in the
private laboratory which he has had built inside what used to be
an old dissecting theatre at the back of his house. In the privacy
of his experiments there he is a radical, espousing new theories
of the interface between mind and body and pushing at the
intellectual boundaries of science; in society, meanwhile, he is a
conventionally philanthropic and church-going conservative. It
is important always to remember that, like all high-functioning
addicts, he is a highly skilled liar...

When reading Jekyll's account of the sheer *pleasure* that his
experiments give him, it is also worth remembering that for the
whole of the three years during which Stevenson lived in the
super-respectable English seaside resort of Bournemouth, where
he wrote the novel, he was taking large doses of medical-grade
morphine to help him deal with his consumption. Morphine
completely untethers you from pain; it makes you feel quite
literally invincible. It is very common, for instance, for patients
receiving morphine to cry with joy only seconds after the
needle has gone in.

And now we come to...

Mr Hyde

The thing about Mr Hyde that everyone agrees on in the novel
is that he is *indefinably* odd. Everyone says he appears to be
inconsequential, slightly built and young – but they insist that
there is something about him that is both curiously upsetting
and profoundly chilling. However, no one is able to say exactly
what it is about him that produces this effect. For instance, they
(and we) never seem to see his face. Eventually, of course, they
(and we) see something that is more or less a psychopathic ape
– a scuttling, gibbering little monster – a non-human – but that
is at the very end of the story, not at its beginning.

At the beginning, Hyde's strongest characteristics are his
detachment, his icy bad manners, his sudden fury – and a strong
whiff of queerness. Utterson, for instance, more or less assumes

that this young man is far more than Jekyll's protégé – a fiction
which Jekyll seems to go along with; Mrs Poole, meanwhile,
seems to think that Sir Danvers Carew may well have been a
closeted homosexual who earned his gruesome end by trying to
chat up the wrong piece of rough trade. Hyde certainly seems to
be weirdly neat and tidy – dapper – and certainly *not* the hairy
monster with buck teeth that he has been portrayed as in a
hundred classic movie posters. (A useful note: Stevenson
himself strongly objected to the portrayal of Jekyll's alter-ego
as a lunatic right from the get-go. This was how it was done in
the first big stage version in London, in 1888; at the Lyceum,
Hyde was a mad sort of hair-covered sex-wolf the very first
time you saw him, and after he had seen this version Stevenson
commented, 'Hyde is no more sexual than the other, but is the
essence of cruelty, and malice, and selfishness, and cowardice,
and these are the diabolic in man.')

So, how does the actor who plays Dr Jekyll also play Mr Hyde?
Well, first they have to accept – and relish – that they must
literally have two bodies in order to play the two roles. After
that, all the clues are there in the original novel. They'll need to
change their clothes; their voice (its class, its rhythm, its
breathiness); their posture and their relation to space – and
especially to change the rhythm of Jekyll's walk into the
alarming little pit-a-pat that Stevenson so brilliantly specifies for
Hyde. It might be wise to add a few key signature accessories –
maybe a dandy's coloured gloves, and/or a vulgar yet neat little
bowler hat to shadow that initially unseen face. The important
thing is that we see a credible little back-street escape artist, not
a senior medical practitioner with the keys to society. It might be
worth looking at pictures of Crippen, or Christie. After all,
neither of them looked like monsters, did they?

And finally...

The original novel is really, I think, about Stevenson exploring,
on the deepest possible personal level, the male violence, the
male privilege, the male addictions and the male guilt that he
felt he had been destined to embody by his upbringing in the

hypocritical and Manichean world of Calvinist Edinburgh. Like that original, this play sets out to probe and dissect the male body. And then, inspired by the fact that Stevenson *did* escape – into a life of quite astonishing freedom and integrity – it asks us what lessons we might want to draw from that dissection.

London
September 2022

This adaptation of *Jekyll and Hyde* was commissioned by
Derby Theatre and Queen's Theatre Hornchurch, and first
performed at Derby Theatre on 30 September 2022 before
transferring to Queen's Theatre Hornchurch, in a Derby Theatre
and Queen's Theatre Hornchurch co-production. The cast was as
follows (in alphabetical order):

DR LANYON	Charlie Buckland
THE MATRON	Hilary Greatorex
THE GIRL	Tife Kusoro
DR STEVENSON	Polly Lister
INSPECTOR NEWCOME	James Morrell
MR ENFIELD	Craig Painting
MR GUEST	Levi Payne
DR JEKYLL / MR HYDE	Nicholas Shaw
MR UTTERSON	Robert Vernon

Director	Sarah Brigham
Designer	Jessica Curtis
Composer and Sound Designer	Ivan Stott
Movement Director	Deb Pugh
Lighting Designer	Simeon Miller
Voice Coach	Anita Gilbert
Casting Director	Kay Magson
Assistant Director	Omar Khan
Magic Consultant	Philip Bond of PMB Theatre & Exhibition Services Ltd
Producers	Stuart Allen (for Derby Theatre) and Mathew Russell (for Queen's Theatre Hornchurch)

Company and Stage Manager	Moby Renshaw
Deputy Stage Manager	Clelia Crawford
Assistant Stage Manager	Anthony Fearnley

JEKYLL AND HYDE

Robert Louis Stevenson

adapted for the stage by
Neil Bartlett

'I have a more subtle opium in my own
mind than any apothecary's drug…'

Robert Louis Stevenson

Characters

DR STEVENSON
THE MATRON
THE GIRL

DR JEKYLL / MR HYDE

THE GENTLEMEN:
   MR ENFIELD
   MR UTTERSON
   DR LANYON
   INSPECTOR NEWCOME
   MR GUEST

Note on Text

Text in bold indicates lines spoken by the chorus of Gentlemen, not necessarily in unison – the choice of which character/actor is speaking is to be worked out during rehearsals.

This text went to press before the end of rehearsals and so may differ slightly from the play as performed.

ACT ONE

Prologue – 'They were always polite...'

DR STEVENSON *is being sworn in as a member of the medical profession in front of* THE GENTLEMEN, *members of an all-male hospital board.*

DR STEVENSON. I swear...

That I will respect the hard-won scientific gains of all those physicians who have come before me, and gladly share all such knowledge as I acquire with those who are to follow me; I swear that I will apply, for the benefit of the sick, all and any measures required.

I swear that I will tread with care in all matters of life and death. Above all, I will not play God.

If I do not violate this my oath, may I enjoy a long life; may I be respected while I live, and remembered with affection thereafter. Long may I experience the joy of healing all who seek my help.

THE GENTLEMEN. **Hear, hear...**

THE GENTLEMEN *applaud – patronisingly – apart from one of them.*

DR STEVENSON *'suspends' the chorus.*

DR STEVENSON. Thank you!

I was the first woman they had ever admitted to their hospital. They were polite, of course – but I knew they were judging me. That they wanted me to fail. In addition to which... well, that whole strange affair of Doctor Jekyll was one of my very first serious cases. It started barely weeks after they'd put me in charge of my first ward –

An iron bell tolls three o'clock. DR STEVENSON *has been putting on her white coat and preparing for a ward-round...*

Late December. A cold night. I'd barely begun my rounds, when we heard screaming...

THE GENTLEMEN *all stay in place – watching – judging – as we dissolve into –*

Scene One – A Cold Night in December

A Victorian hospital ward, 3 a.m.

DR STEVENSON *examines* THE GIRL, *trying to find out what has happened to her. A flurry of action. A trolley – a screen. The* MATRON *takes charge, bringing* THE GIRL *a blanket, holding an enamel pan in case she needs to vomit, etc.* THE GIRL *is furious, she is very badly bruised and has a nosebleed.*

THE GIRL. Why didn't 'e stop? Why didn't 'e stop? He bloody 'urt me.

MATRON. Doctor, she seems to saying that somebody walked on her. *Trampled* her, I think she said.

THE GIRL (*exhibiting her bruises*). Well, what d'you think those are, bloody Scotch mist?

DR STEVENSON (*examining her methodically*). Nothing broken... No other bleeding that I can see. I think she's mostly just scared...

THE GIRL. Well, wouldn't you be? Out of bloody nowhere – Ow!

DR STEVENSON (*to* MATRON, *as she continues her examination*). Any witnesses?

THE GIRL (*suspicious – is she going to call the police?*). What d'you mean, 'witnesses'? I told you –

MATRON (*to* THE GIRL). The doctor means, can anybody corroborate?

THE GIRL. What?

DR STEVENSON. Was there anybody else there who might have seen who attacked you?

THE GIRL (*defensive*). No.

DR STEVENSON (*still checking* THE GIRL*'s injuries*). So nobody but you can give us the information we might need to make sure this doesn't happen to someone else.

THE GIRL. Yes. I mean no. Ow! There was one person. A gentleman. 'E saw what 'appened.

MR ENFIELD *leaves the chorus of* GENTLEMEN *and joins the scene.*

ENFIELD (*interrupting*). Excuse me, miss! Miss, I – Certainly there was a witness.

MATRON (*to* THE GIRL). Is this him?

THE GIRL. Is this 'im, what?

MATRON. Is this the gentlemen who saw you being hurt?

THE GIRL. Well, why don't you ask him? Bet he don't tell you though.

DR STEVENSON (*to* MATRON). Just a wash and dress please, Matron. Try and keep her quiet – and find her something clean to put on, if you can –

DR STEVENSON *isn't being deliberately rude, but it is gone 3 a.m. and she is working – so during this conversation she is busy washing her hands, writing up notes, checking what the next job is in her rounds, etc.*

(*To* ENFIELD.) And you are?

ENFIELD. Mister Richard Enfield, miss. I –

DR STEVENSON. Doctor.

ENFIELD. Sorry? Oh, I see. Richard Enfield, doctor, at your service.

DR STEVENSON (*checking her watch, tired*). Good morning. Well, did you?

ENFIELD. Did I what?

DR STEVENSON. See who did this to that girl?

Beat.

ENFIELD. Well, it was this way, mi– doctor –

He is not quite sure how to address her, never having met a female doctor before.

I was coming home…

DR STEVENSON. At three o'clock in the morning.

ENFIELD. Exactly – and it's a black night – and I have to say that's a part of town where there is *literally* nothing to be seen but lamps – streets as empty as a church. I tell you, I was quite longing for the sight of a policemen –

DR STEVENSON. What were you doing in an 'empty' part of town, Mister Enfield, making your way home at three o'clock in the morning? If you don't mind me asking.

ENFIELD. I'd rather not say.

THE GIRL (*possibly behind a screen, where she is being attended to by* MATRON). Told ya!

MATRON. Hold still.

THE GIRL. Ow!

DR STEVENSON. I see. And can anyone vouch for this story?

ENFIELD. Well, I – Good heavens.

MR UTTERSON *comes to join him.*

UTTERSON. All right, Enfield?! Utterson, doctor – of Utterson and Osborne –

You've probably heard the name. Currently one of the *senior* legal firms of Lincoln's Inn…

He presents DR STEVENSON *with his card, which she inspects.*

…Mister Enfield here has been of my acquaintance for several years. I assure you, you can take him entirely at his word.

THE GIRL emerges from behind the screen, doing up a hospital gown.

THE GIRL. Ask him about the corner.

DR STEVENSON. Thank you. Matron!

She indicates to MATRON to keep THE GIRL out of the way – and checks UTTERSON's card.

Thank you for speaking up, Mister... Utterson. (*To ENFIELD.*) So, sir, you were longing for a policeman –

ENFIELD. Yes, I was. And that was when I saw them.

DR STEVENSON. 'Them'? Just a minute please.

She starts to take notes – which THE GENTLMEN don't like...

Carry on.

ENFIELD. Right. One figure was a man – a *little* man, stumping along at rather a good walk – coming round a corner – and the other was this girl here – *running*, I might say – at that time of night – and in *that* part of town.

THE GIRL. So?

MATRON. Sssh.

THE GIRL. Don't you shush me!

DR STEVENSON. Thank you, Mister Enfield.

ENFIELD. And then, the two of them arrived simultaneously in front of this funny old black *door* – Oh!

DR STEVENSON. Yes?

ENFIELD. Actually, Utterson, you know this door – we passed it last time we were out, er... walking together. You remember – a rather sordid, distained sort of a *back* door it was. Distinctly... neglected. No bell or knocker anywhere. You remarked on it...

UTTERSON is clearly uneasy – which DR STEVENSON notices.

UTTERSON. Yes... Yes, I do remember you pointing out something of that kind. Rather a dingy neighbourhood, as I recall.

ENFIELD. Indeed – where was I?

DR STEVENSON. You were about to tell us what happened to the child.

ENFIELD. Ah yes – so. I was passing this rather sordid-looking door, this *back* door, as I say – and the little man was coming round one side of the corner – and this young lady was running round hers, and then... well...

He enlists support.

– I say, gentlemen, would you mind?

THE GENTLEMEN *all now join* ENFIELD – *apart from the one who didn't clap, who stays sitting, alone and silent (we will discover later who this is).*

THE GENTLEMEN (*oddly hearty*). Not at all, Mister Enfield –

Glad to be of assistance, sir – (*Etc.*)

Under ENFIELD's *supervision – this should be all a bit ad lib – the other* GENTLEMEN *help him to reconstruct the assault as you would in courtroom. They do it rather clumsily, but with some enthusiasm and self-importance – the occasional jacket may come off, for instance.* DR STEVENSON *takes notes throughout.*

ENFIELD. Right. Thank you, gentlemen. So, the little man's coming round one side of the corner, stumping – and she's coming round the other one – running – and the door was sort of here – in the middle – and so naturally when they reached it –

THE GIRL. 'Ang on.

MATRON. Miss, please!

ENFIELD. I beg your pardon?

THE GIRL. Well, you've only gone and got it the wrong way round, ain't yer – I was coming round that way. So the er little one or whatever must 'ave been coming round opposite.

D'y'see?

ENFIELD. As you say. Gentlemen?

They rearrange themselves, swapping left for right, and the reconstruction continues.

So – if I may – man – girl – there we are – yes? – door – stumping – running – corner – there we go: bang! – and then – and this was the peculiar and actually rather horrible part of the thing, the child's quite right, he trampled her. Instead of stopping he walked – and I mean to say, *calmly* – right over the child's body – while she was screaming blue murder.

THE GIRL. Too bloody right I was.

ENFIELD. I mean it wasn't like a man, it was more like some sort of damned juggernaut.

The reconstruction has developed into a bizarre and image: one of THE GENTLEMEN *has been lifted high in the air by the others so that his feet are cycling in the air. The picture is horrible – and clumsy – but all quite clinical, as if we were indeed in a courtroom.* DR STEVENSON *is taking detailed notes – and also clearly wondering why* UTTERSON *isn't watching, but rather turned away and deep in thought about something…*

THE GIRL. Never mind juggerthingy, he was all bloody over me. Just like I said, doctor.

ENFIELD. As the young lady says. And the thing was – when I confronted the little… gentleman – collared him, if you really want to know – actually literally grabbed him – he –

DR STEVENSON. Yes?

ENFIELD. He was perfectly cool about the whole business – made no resistance or anything. Which was rather – well, it seemed –

He is clearly disconcerted by remembering his sensations at this point… slightly sweaty.

UTTERSON. All right there, Enfield?

ENFIELD. Oh yes. It was just that he made me rather feel as if I wanted to… strike him. You know? Which was very odd. Sorry. Thank you, gentlemen.

THE GENTLEMEN *disassemble whatever tableau they had created, and start to put their jackets back on and head back to their seats, when –*

DR STEVENSON. And might you be able to say what this odd or little man looked like, Mister Enfield?

ENFIELD. What?

DR STEVENSON. What sort of man was he to see? I'd like to pass a description on to the police.

He hesitates – wipes away some sweat with a handkerchief.

ENFIELD. Well, er… he was… he –

THE GIRL. 'E had this face, see. And it was all sort of. When 'e looked at you. It made you feel like you were all sort of – like you was really cold. Sorry, miss.

Chorus One – 'What sort of man was he to see?'

Public-school voices… THE GIRL, in the middle of this, searches for her missing memory. She is intimidated – but also angry. Why can't she remember her assailant? Why does he elude her?

THE SIXTH GENTLEMAN (*in a silky whisper*). He was actually rather hard to describe…

THE OTHER GENTLEMEN (*variously*). **Yes I noticed that –**

Me too –

THE GIRL. Yeah, but 'e was definitely –

THE GENTLEMEN (*interrupting*). **Oh there was definitely something *wrong* about him –**

Wrong with his *appearance*, I mean –

Oh, downright detestable, if you ask me...

THE GIRL. Right – and there was this crowd, miss – this whole crowd, right round us –

THE GENTLEMEN. **And when he gave you that look of his –**

(*Deliberately scaring her.*) **Hah!**

THE GIRL. That's it!

THE GENTLEMEN. **It was as if...**

THE GIRL. Go on –

THE GENTLEMEN. **Well, it was so ugly, it certainly brought *me* out in a sweat.**

THE GIRL. What about 'is eyes? 'E 'ad these eyes, miss – they –

THE GENTLEMEN (*interrrupting again*). **Yes, the eyes were chilling...**

Yes that's it –

Disgusting...

I'd say it was rather as if he didn't *have* a face.

THE GIRL. But 'e must 'ave. Ev'rybody 'as a *face*!

THE GENTLEMEN *turn on her with a snarl.*

THE GENTLEMEN. **Really?!**

Wisely, THE GIRL *backs off. Left in control of the space,* THE GENTLEMEN*'s upper-class confidence begins to curdle into display of boorish, public-schoolboy aggression –*

So... I told him we'd make such a scandal out of this –

Make his name stink from one end of London to the other –

**If he had any friends, I said, he'd better get ready to
bloody lose 'em –**

That's right!

The voices bray and go sour. THE GIRL *gets out of it and
goes to be with* DR STEVENSON – *making sure she is
getting the story down correctly.*

**Meanwhile of course the girl's family were going
absolutely wild –**

THE GIRL. That was my mum, miss.

THE GENTLEMEN. **Absolute bloody harpies –**

**I mean, I had to keep one woman off him with my own
bloody hands –**

When THE GENTLEMEN *do Hyde's voice, they fully
impersonate him, mimicking the fact that he is a lower class
than they are.*

**And – 'No gentleman but wishes to avoid a scene' – he
says –**

THE GIRL. That's right –

THE GENTLEMEN. **'Name your figure' – he says –**

Frightened, of course – you could see that –

But with this kind of sneering sort of a coolness to him –

And I tell you, it made you want to –

I mean, it really made you want to – you know – to –

*They look like they want to hurt or even kill the figure they
are remembering – a really ugly tableau of masculine
aggression.*

So we screwed him!

We screwed the bastard –

For a hundred bloody pounds –

A hundred!

THE GIRL. That's true, miss – a bloody hundred.

THE GENTLEMEN. **Come on, we said.**

Pay up, you filthy, sneering, sick-making little –

And so anyway, he turns round –

He whips out a bloody key –

And he disappears right through that bloody door.

D'you see? Absolutely bloody vanishes…

D'you see?

Beat.

THE SIXTH GENTLEMAN. Oh, I'm sure she does…

THE GENTLEMEN *are panting, trying to recover themselves…*

DR STEVENSON *is wondering who that* SIXTH GENTLEMAN *is and what he's got to do with all this…*

THE GIRL (*quoting the familiar call from a pantomime*). Oh no he wasn't!

MATRON. Wasn't what, dear?

THE GIRL. Vanished. (*To* THE GENTLEMEN.) 'E came right back out again. And – go on, tell 'er what 'e 'ad in his 'and already.

No one moves…

MATRON. The girl says her attacker came back, gentlemen.

DR STEVENSON (*having been distracted by her thoughts*). Sorry. Gentlemen?

THE GENTLEMEN *consider – then lurch back into action. They play that the odd little man is suddenly there again.*

THE GENTLEMEN. **Oh yes. He came back all right – through the door –**

Holding a bloody cheque from *Coutts bank*, **would you mind –**

We see the cheque being passed around.

Payable to bearer, obviously – and –

(*Spotting the signature.*) **Hang on –**

What?

Oh good Lord.

Let me see… good Lord.

That cheque was bloody signed all right, miss…

The cheque is passed to UTTERSON, *so he can see the signature too – but he passes it on without looking at it –*

UTTERSON. Yes I imagine it was.

THE GENTLEMEN. **Well, we said… thank you very much –**

And that was that. We took it round to Coutts – and her mother got her hundred quid by breakfast time. A hundred…

bloody…

quid… (*Pointedly.*) **doctor.**

Scene Two – 'Yes, but what about that cheque?'

Reconstruction of the crime over, three of the GENTLEMEN *return to their seats, leaving* UTTERSON *and* ENFIELD *as before…*

DR STEVENSON *is busy finishing her notes and does not look up.*

DR STEVENSON. Yes, thank you, I think that's everything. Matron, would you…? (*Indicating that she is to escort them out.*)

MATRON. Of course, doctor. Gentlemen?

DR STEVENSON (*catching them just before they exit –
offhand*). Sorry – just one more thing. What *was* the name on
the cheque, Mister Enfield?

ENFIELD. One I shan't mention, if you don't mind.

DR STEVENSON. Because?

ENFIELD. Because answering that sort of a question partakes
too much of judgement. You start with a question, and the
next thing you know, you're judging a feller. Besides, the
more it looks like Queer Street, the less a gentleman asks.
In my opinion.

DR STEVENSON. I'm sure. Thank you anyway, Mister
Enfield, and goodnight... Matron.

DR STEVENSON *goes back her notes – and of course* THE
GIRL *and* MATRON *have realised how cleverly* DR
STEVENSON *is playing these men by apparently letting
them off the hook. We see* MATRON *signal to* THE GIRL
not to interrupt, and then usher the men away from DR
STEVENSON. UTTERSON *and* ENFIELD *speak their next
dialogue quietly – as if they were in a corridor just outside
the ward, perhaps – and foolishly assume that they therefore
won't be overhead.*

UTTERSON. Enfield!

ENFIELD. Yes?

UTTERSON. Was that correct?

ENFIELD. Was what?

UTTERSON. That this man used a key.

ENFIELD. My dear sir –

UTTERSON (*angrily insisting*). You're absolutely sure he had a
key to that back door?

ENFIELD. Yes, the fellow had a key – and I say, Utterson –
(*Conspiratorially.*) between you and me – he'd got that
cheque of his signed by – well by a somebody rather
celebrated. A proper top-end do-gooder, if you get my drift.

So, Blackmail House, I should say, might be what lies behind that black back door. Mum's the word, eh?

UTTERSON. Quite.

They shake hands on it.

(*Offhand.*) Did you catch the other man's name?

ENFIELD. Sorry?

UTTERSON. The man who trampled the child.

ENFIELD. Called himself Edward, I think. Yes, that's it: Edward Hyde.

Beat.

UTTERSON. I beg your pardon?

ENFIELD. Hyde, sir. The man told us his name was Edward Hyde.

UTTERSON. I see. Thank you, Enfield...

ENFIELD. Not at all...

ENFIELD *is dismissed and begins to return to his seat amongst* THE GENTLEMEN. UTTERSON *seems poleaxed – not that* ENFIELD *noticed.* DR STEVENSON *is still scribbling.*

THE GIRL (*making sure they all hear her*). Did you get all that, miss?

DR STEVENSON. Yes. (*Calling after him.*) Thank you, Mister Enfield. You've been most helpful.

THE GIRL (*ironically calling after him as well, mimicking* DR STEVENSON). Thank you, Mister Enfield... (*As herself.*) Safe home, dear!

ENFIELD. Well, really!

He returns to his seat.

Scene Three – 'Not *the* Doctor Jekyll?'

DR STEVENSON. Mister Utterson – if you've still got a moment –

UTTERSON. Yes?

DR STEVENSON. I wouldn't wish to seem impertinent, sir, but I wonder if *you* might by any chance have recognised the signature on that cheque.

UTTERSON *pulls all available ranks – class, profession, age and gender.*

UTTERSON. And how exactly could I have recognised something I never saw? You forget I wasn't there.

Beat.

DR STEVENSON. Obviously, but I didn't ask if you'd seen it, Mister Utterson, I asked merely if you might have recognised it if you had...

THE GENTLEMEN *are all ears.*

UTTERSON. All right.

I imagine the signature would have belonged to a Doctor Henry Jekyll.

Beat. UTTERSON *thinks from the expression on* DR STEVENSON*'s face that she hasn't understood – or perhaps hasn't heard of him.*

Henry Jekyll MD. Fellow of the Royal Society? – Close friend of mine. Also a client, in my legal capacity as his solicitor.

DR STEVENSON. Not *the* Doctor Jekyll, sir?

UTTERSON. Yes. Why?

DR STEVENSON. I've read several of his recent papers – on the roots of identity. I think they're... extraordinary.

UTTERSON. That, doctor, I'm not qualified to judge.

This mention of Jekyll has clearly changed everything for
DR STEVENSON. *He is evidently one of her medical heroes.*

DR STEVENSON. Why on earth would you think the signature might be Henry Jekyll's, Mister Utterson?

UTTERSON – *realising that there is no going back, and perhaps that this young woman is no more a fool than he is – produces some legal-looking papers, and finds the relevant page.*

UTTERSON. Because of the name given to Enfield by this wretched girl's assailant.

DR STEVENSON. I don't follow.

UTTERSON (*snapping*). No, evidently you don't, doctor. However, I shall *attempt* to explain. I keep in my safe a copy of the aforementioned Henry Jekyll's will – a will which he has recently asked me to alter.

Beat. UTTERSON *is leafing through the document.*

DR STEVENSON. How?

UTTERSON. By inserting a final clause which will ensure that in the case of his decease or disappearance his entire estate – his *entire* estate, please note – will pass into the hands of his friend, Mister Edward Hyde. Paragraph fourteen.

DR STEVENSON (*scanning*). Fourteen…

THE GIRL. And what does that mean, when it's at home?

DR STEVENSON *is studying the will.*

MATRON. Sssh, the doctor's just reading it to find out.

THE GIRL. I can see what she's doin', but I want to know what it –

MATRON. We all do. You'll just have to be patient.

THE GIRL. Oh, right…

DR STEVENSON. I imagine that for a lawyer, this word 'disappearance' is rather an eyesore.

UTTERSON. The whole clause is an offence to sanity –

DR STEVENSON. Then I don't understand.

UTTERSON (*massively condescending*). What, specifically?

Beat

DR STEVENSON. Why, when Mister Enfield recounted his story – sir – you forgot to mention that you already knew Hyde's name.

Longer beat.

THE GIRL. My mum said what *she* don't understand is 'ow anyone can unlock a tatty old door then come straight back out with a hundred knicker...

UTTERSON. Then tell your mother it's because that door...

A pause. Ominous sound. THE SIXTH GENTLEMAN *stirs...*

...that door is in fact the back door to Harry... I mean Doctor Jekyll... to his house.

DR STEVENSON *and* MATRON *begin to realise just how much might be wrong here.* UTTERSON *is realising just how far this is spinning out of control...* THE SIXTH GENTLEMAN *and his team also seem very concerned.*

THE GIRL. Pull the other one...

MATRON. Will you be quiet?!

DR STEVENSON. So we are on Queer Street. I see.

UTTERSON. Do you, miss?

Look: Harry practises... I mean, he conducts experiments, sometimes, in an old dissecting theatre at the rear of his premises –

DR STEVENSON. – to which he has given this 'friend' of his a key –

UTTERSON. Yes –

DR STEVENSON. A 'friend' who you – and I – know to be capable of real foulness –

UTTERSON. I told him it was madness –

THE GENTLEMEN *emit a strange hissing sound, like a cornered animal baring its teeth –*

DR STEVENSON. This isn't madness, Mister Utterson – he's given him a key, he signs him cheques. I'm afraid your client is exposing himself to – to –

UTTERSON (*cutting her off and daring her to complete the accusation*). To what? Yes?

DR STEVENSON. To the slow cancer of disgrace.

After a nasty silence, THE SIXTH GENTLEMAN *and his bully-boys echo her line.*

THE GENTLEMEN. **Disgrace!**

Cutting the scene, a voice which we haven't heard yet – DR LANYON.

Scene Four – An Intervention

LANYON. Hear, hear! And you aren't the only one with suspicions – Lanyon, doctor – Professor Hastie Lanyon, Royal College of Surgeons retired –

DR STEVENSON. Professor –

LANYON. – also a sometime friend of this damned Harry Jekyll's. Three of us went to the same school, wouldn't you know. Utterson –

They shake hands.

But once he'd begun to publish – well, the man had clearly begun to go wrong – and some of the most recent speculations – on these experiments of his – *most* unscientific, in my opinion. I continued to take an interest in him – to dine, occasionally, for old's sake, as they say – but approve of the man, no. Always thought he had a slyish cast about the face... That's all.

UTTERSON. Have you ever heard Harry mention this Hyde fellow, Hastie?

LANYON. Who?

UTTERSON. Hyde – younger man, seems to be some sort of a protégé of his.

LANYON. Never heard of him. Since my time. Carry on, doctor. Carry on. Oh –

Realising that, as a doctor, he owes her the professional courtesy of a handshake before he goes, LANYON *awkwardly holds out his hand.* DR STEVENSON *suspends the scene.*

DR STEVENSON. Thank you!

(*To the audience.*) Rest assured, I did. Carry on. But... the trail went cold. No connection between Jekyll and the man who'd assaulted the girl could be proved. The girl's injuries healed, and I was rather busy with learning my new profession.

MATRON *takes advantage of the suspension to do a quick spot of tidying up.*

MATRON. You did very well, doctor. Top marks.

DR STEVENSON. Thank you. And then – and as I remember it this was four or even five whole weeks later – Utterson unexpectedly turned up at the hospital.

MATRON (*seeing their unexpected visitor*). Doctor –

DR STEVENSON. Mister Utterson – can I help?

UTTERSON (*unsure, diminished*). Perhaps.

He takes a deep breath, and commits to unlocking the suspension and continuing with the story.

Yes. Thank you.

LANYON *returns to his seat. We should not notice that* THE SIXTH GENTLEMAN *leaves his seat and exits at this point.* UTTERSON *gets out his handkerchief and mops his brow.*

DR STEVENSON. Do you need to sit down, Mister Utterson? A glass of water?

The other GENTLEMEN *are perhaps mimicking his brow-mopping gesture – a weird rippling echo…* MATRON *fetches the water.*

THE GIRL (*to* MATRON). He don't look very well, does 'e?

MATRON. No.

UTTERSON (*popping a pill with his water*). Thank you. I haven't been sleeping too well. Customarily, I am of Cain's heresy –

THE GIRL. Beg pardon?

UTTERSON. – let your brother go to the devil after his own way, all of that malarkey… but after Enfield's story, doctor – well, I found I kept on seeing this girl. At night. Girls, actually… being trodden on. By that creature of Henry's.

DR STEVENSON. And have you *done* anything about these… dreams of yours, Mister Utterson?

UTTERSON. Such as?

DR STEVENSON. Confronting Doctor Jekyll about his choice of 'friend'.

UTTERSON. No – but last night I did remember something *I* learnt, when I was starting: 'What else does one do with a mystery, but examine it?' No man *is* without a face, is he – and if this young man of Henry's be Mister Hyde, then I thought perhaps I ought to be Mister Seek…

Thank you!

At this instruction, a change in light and sound takes us to the next scene – the iron bell begins to toll again, perhaps a Gothic full moon…

Now if you could just give me a hand… I think this time we'll use an actual door…

With the help of DR STEVENSON, MATRON *and* THE
GIRL, UTTERSON *sets up the shabby back door of Jekyll's
house – very much in the same spirit of reconstruction as
earlier. The door gets spun round while it is being set up, so
that we can see there is nothing on the other side of it. We do
not see that, somewhere in this set-up,* MATRON *goes to get
something from behind a screen (for instance) and does not
return.* UTTERSON, *meanwhile, dons a cape or coat.*

Scene Five – London Went Very Silent

A freezing night, early January.

UTTERSON. I'd been haunting that shabby back door of
Jekyll's for two whole weeks. Nothing.

He acts being very cold: stamping, blowing on hands, etc.

THE GIRL (*sarcastically*). Gets parky standing out on a street
corner all night, don't it, sir? In January.

UTTERSON. I found that to be the case, certainly.

THE GIRL. Oh, did ya? And?

UTTERSON. And – finally – sssh –

THE GENTLEMEN *whistle the opening bars of Hyde's
insidious little tune – 'Maybe It's Because I'm a Londoner'
by Hubert Gregg.*

I'd been at my post some time – the streets were as clean as a
ballroom floor – when London went very silent all of a
sudden –

THE GENTLEMEN *stop –*

And I was somehow *sure –*

THE GIRL. Oh, I don't like this. I don't like it, doctor.

UTTERSON. Get her out of the way, will you?

THE GIRL. It's 'im again, ain't it –

DR STEVENSON. The gentleman's only telling a story – Matron!

THE GIRL *is passed over to* MATRON. *The whistling resumes. Footsteps, getting louder: sharp, pattering, maimed-sounding…*

A small, neat and slightly oddly shaped man enters from nowhere and walks towards the door. Whereas everyone else so far has been dressed as a gentleman, he looks different. He walks with an odd, light, pit-a-pat footstep – and as if he was heading home after a night out. He is whistling under his breath – the same tune THE GENTLEMEN *were whistling just now. He gets out his keys.*

UTTERSON. Mister Hyde.

HYDE *immediately shrinks back in fear, hissing like an animal –* THE GENTLEMEN *echo the same sound and gesture – but only for a moment.*

HYDE (*recovering*). That is my name. What do *you* want?

UTTERSON. I'm an old friend of Henry Jekyll's. Utterson.

HYDE. And?

UTTERSON. I see you're dropping in to visit Henry – perhaps you might admit me as well?

HYDE. You won't find Doctor Jekyll in. He's… away.

UTTERSON. Where?

HYDE. From home.

HYDE *blows on the key.*

How did you know me?

UTTERSON. If Harry's out, will you perhaps do me a favour anyway?

HYDE. Oh, with pleasure, what shall it be?

UTTERSON. Let me see your face.

HYDE *shows his face to* UTTERSON *for a few seconds. We don't see it.* THE GENTLEMEN *bare their teeth and hiss.* THE GIRL *tries to see, but is restrained by* DR STEVENSON *and* MATRON.

UTTERSON. Now I shall know you again. Should that ever be required.

HYDE. As you say. In fact… Utterson… why don't you have my address. It's14, Meard Street. Soho. Just in case you ever need to contact me in a hurry… over anything *legal*.

UTTERSON (*alarmed by this reference to the will*). What?! What d'you mean, 'in a hurry'?

HYDE (*mocking his loss of cool*). Oops! Steady on… Utterson.

How *did* you know me, by the way?

UTTERSON. By description.

HYDE. Whose?

UTTERSON. We have common friends.

HYDE (*a little hoarsely*). Do we? Who are they?

UTTERSON. Doctor Henry Jekyll, for one.

HYDE (*sudden anger – then laughter*). *He* never mentioned me! Oh, Mister Utterson, I did not think you would have *lied* –

UTTERSON. Come, sir, that is not fitting language –

HYDE. See you in Soho – sir –

HYDE *laughs – and nips in through the door. We hear it being locked from the inside – and see* UTTERSON *try the door handle, but to no avail. We should be sure* HYDE *is very definitely locked in behind the door.*

Scene Six – 'Is Doctor Jekyll at home?'

THE GIRL. You let him go? What was you bloody thinking?!

DR STEVENSON. Yes, what were you thinking, Mister Utterson?

UTTERSON (*near exploding*). I was thinking, miss – that snide, sneering little *thing*, for a 'friend'? Good God, Harry.

THE GIRL. Well, I tell ya, I wouldn't leave him nuffink in *my* will –

UTTERSON. Exactly! Exactly… So…

A beat of indecision.

DR STEVENSON. We're waiting, Mister Utterson –

THE GIRL. We certainly are, mister.

UTTERSON. Yes. Right.

UTTERSON *makes a decision. He grabs the door and turns it. The reverse side of the back door has somehow turned into the front door of Jekyll's house. Shiny paint, big shiny doorknocker, visibly posh.*

I walked round to the front of the house… which as you can see was on a different kind of street altogether – no stains or shabbiness in *that* part of town – and knocked.

No one moves. It seems that no one knows what is next in the story. UTTERSON *knocks again.*

Hello? Harry, it's –

Cracking the tension, the door opens – but it isn't who it ought to be, i.e. Hyde… No – he has apparently vanished, and it is MATRON (*playing* MRS POOLE *the housekeeper*) *who comes out through the door. She plays that we are now inside the house.*

MRS POOLE. Good evening, sir.

THE GIRL *responds to the unexpectedness of this entrance, wondering both how did* MATRON *get behind that door, and why is she playing this character…*

THE GIRL. What?

UTTERSON *plays completely within the scene, with no surprise at all.*

UTTERSON. Good evening, Mrs Poole, is Doctor Jekyll at home?

MRS POOLE (*taking his hat and coat*). I'll just go and see, Mister Utterson – I think he's out back in his laboratory. Shall you wait here by the library fire, sir, or shall I give you a light in the doctor's dining room?

UTTERSON. Here will be fine, thank you.

MRS POOLE. Very good, sir.

MRS POOLE *leaves the room.*

UTTERSON. Normally I liked that room – firelight – polish – but not tonight. Encountering that squalid little creature in the flesh had really –

MRS POOLE (*returning*). Doctor Jekyll must have gone out, sir.

UTTERSON. I see. Thank you, Poole.

MRS POOLE. Well, goodnight, sir.

UTTERSON. Yes. By the way, I just met a Mister Hyde going in through the *back* door here – into Harry's old dissecting theatre. Is that right, when the doctor's out?

MRS POOLE. Mister Hyde has a key, sir.

UTTERSON. Your master seems to repose a great deal of trust in this particular young man.

MRS POOLE (*uncomfortable*). We all have orders to obey Mister Hyde, sir.

UTTERSON. Yet I don't think I've ever *met* him here. Socially.

MRS POOLE. Oh dear, sir, no – Mister Hyde never *dines* here. He mostly comes and goes by the laboratory side of things, sir, we see very little of him on this side of the house.

UTTERSON. I see. Well, goodnight, Poole.

MRS POOLE. Goodnight, sir.

THE GENTLEMEN (*in Hyde's voice – hostile, sneering*). **Goodnight...** *sir.*

MATRON *doesn't go out through the door again, she simply steps out of role – takes off her apron of whatever – and becomes herself again. She keeps a very close eye on* UTTERSON *in the next scene to see if her contribution has moved him any closer to telling her colleague* DR STEVENSON *what she needs to know.*

Scene Seven – Losing Patience

DR STEVENSON *is losing patience with* UTTERSON.

DR STEVENSON (*replying to that sneering voice of intimidation*). Thank you, gentlemen... And don't tell me, Mister Utterson – you went home –

UTTERSON (*getting out his hip flask*). Yes –

DR STEVENSON. And you thought – well, if it *is* disgrace – I mean if this Hyde creature *is* blackmailing my highly valued client in some way – well – we were all wild when we were young –

THE GENTLEMEN-HYDES. **Oh hear, hear...**

UTTERSON *takes a swig from a hip flask, and pops another pill.*

DR STEVENSON. We all have the odd 'sin' behind us – why, I imagine even you yourself, Mister Utterson, back in the day –

UTTERSON. What?

DR STEVENSON. But surely this Hyde person – Hyde must have secrets compared to which Harry's would be like sunshine. I mean, Hyde sounds hardly a *gentleman*...

THE GENTLEMEN *give their Hyde-like hiss of alarm*...

UTTERSON (*suddenly struck*). Oh, Lord! What if...

THE GIRL. What? What is it?

THE GENTLEMEN-HYDES *hiss again. They are furious that* DR STEVENSON *is getting close*...

DR STEVENSON. Exactly, Mister Utterson. What if Hyde knows about the clause in Harry's will...

UTTERSON (*bluffing*). Yes. But... Why would that matter?

DR STEVENSON. Because he might grow impatient to inherit. Because he has a key to Harry's house –

UTTERSON *looks at the door in panic – and we should be reminded that we don't know where Hyde went to or where he might be now.* THE GENTLEMEN-HYDES *lean in – we hear that tune again... and now it sounds diabolical... lascivious*...

Can you imagine, sir? That *thing* – in the doctor's house. At night. Bending over the doctor's bed...

THE GENTLEMEN-HYDES. **Aaaaah!**

DR STEVENSON. If you could only get your client to talk to you. I'm sure he'd explain...

UTTERSON (*cracking*). He did. He did explain.

DR STEVENSON (*ready with her notebook for the details*). All right. When?

UTTERSON. Only in a manner of speaking, you understand –

DR STEVENSON. I'll try.

Beat.

UTTERSON. It was fortnight later. I'd been invited to dine –
and Harry always kept rather a good cellar, so I –

DR STEVENSON (*wanting him to get to the point*). Mister
Utterson?

UTTERSON. Yes?

DR STEVENSON. I think this might be easier if you just show
us.

UTTERSON (*defeated*). Of course. Thank you!

Scene Eight – Port and Cigars

A fortnight later, Chez Jekyll.

*Lights change – and suddenly there is hearty round of masculine
laughter from* THE GENTLEMEN *– as if a joke had just been
made over port and cigars at an all-male dinner party. On strolls*
THE SIXTH GENTELMAN *– who is, of course,* DR JEKYLL *–
in immaculate evening dress. We are mid-discussion.*

JEKYLL. I see your point, my dear Utterson, honestly I do –
but I'm not at all sure that we're any of us capable of being
defined by *appearance*.

UTTERSON. But surely, Harry, a man's *face* –

JEKYLL. – is his facade. Science alone can illuminate a man's
true nature.

LANYON. Science, sir?! Is that what you call these latest
experiments of yours?

JEKYLL. Oh, come, Professor Lanyon, surely even you agree
that one has a duty to shine the light of enquiry on this
particular question –

LANYON. Within professional limits, sir!

A pause. LANYON *got a little heated there.*

UTTERSON. What question, Harry?

JEKYLL. That of war between the differing elements of a single nature.

THE GENTLEMEN (*trying to fill a silence*). Oh, hear, hear...

Another pause.

UTTERSON. Carry on, Harry.

JEKYLL. I believe...

LANYON. Do you, sir?

JEKYLL. I believe that others will come after us – that they will outstrip our current state of knowledge – and that one day we will come to understand that not only do two basic and conflicting natures contend in the field of every human consciousness, but that man will ultimately be known to contain multitudes –

LANYON. Oh good Lord –

JEKYLL. – and that every mind – every *body* – will one day be known as a polity of multifarious, incongruous and quite possibly *independent* citizens.

LANYON. Oh, come now, Jekyll –

JEKYLL. Professor Lanyon, I would remind you that steam and electricity were once sneered at as modern impossibilities.

After a moment, laughter erupts again and the moment of tension passes.

THE GENTLEMEN. Hear, hear!

Bravo, Jekyll!

Well said, Henry...

Applause. LANYON, exasperated, throws down his napkin, which suspends the scene.

Scene Nine – 'About this will of yours…'

After dinner.

JEKYLL *and* UTTERSON *are now alone.*

JEKYLL. Well, my friend, dinner is over. What is it you wished to say to me?

UTTERSON. About this will of yours –

JEKYLL. My dear man, you seem as distressed by that new clause as our arch-pedant Lanyon is by my current experiments –

UTTERSON. You know I never approved of its wording –

JEKYLL. Yes, you said –

UTTERSON. Well, now I say it again. The fact is, I have been learning something of this young Mister Hyde of yours –

JEKYLL. I thought we'd agreed to drop that subject –

UTTERSON. – and what I've heard is abominable, Harry. Abominable…

JEKYLL. You don't understand my position. And this is not an affair that can be mended by talking.

UTTERSON. Harry, whatever it is, I have no doubt I can get you out of it.

THE GENTLEMEN, *it seems, are not as 'suspended' as we thought. Heads turn, threateningly…*

JEKYLL. Utterson, that's so good of you – but it really isn't what you fancy – honestly it's not – and to put your good heart at rest, I tell you, the moment I choose, I can be rid of young Mister Hyde *entirely* – and I'll just add one final word, that I'm sure you'll take in good part, which is that this is a private matter, and as an old and trusted friend, I do beg of you to let it sleep.

UTTERSON. Funny you should mention sleep, Harry…

A pause.

JEKYLL. I know you've seen him.

UTTERSON. What?

JEKYLL. He told me – and also that he was rather rude. But – rudeness notwithstanding – I do sincerely take a very great interest in this young man – and his future – and if – *if* – I am ever taken unexpectedly away –

UTTERSON. Harry!

JEKYLL. I ask you to promise – as my lawyer – that you will help Mister Hyde to obtain his full legal and financial rights. I should so hate him to be without money, you see.

Well?

UTTERSON. Very well. As your lawyer, I promise.

JEKYLL. You dear man. Now… let us drop the matter entirely –

JEKYLL holds out his hand – but UTTERSON doesn't have time to take it.

DR STEVENSON (*intervening suddenly*). Yes, thank you!

The lights change, the suspension shifts. DR STEVENSON walks into the scene. JEKYLL is now the one who is suspended.

Scene Ten – 'Did you not, in fact, suspect…'

During this next scene THE GENTLEMEN all turn their (hostile) focus on DR STEVENSON.

DR STEVENSON. Mister Utterson – again, I hope you don't mind me asking – but how much approximately was Doctor Jekyll worth?

UTTERSON. Approximately, a quarter of a million sterling.

THE GIRL. Bloody 'ell!

DR STEVENSON. Be quiet! And just to be clear, you were already wondering, were you not, what exactly that word '*disappearance*' might óne day refer to?

UTTERSON. Yes, but I –

DR STEVENSON. But nothing. Did you not in fact suspect that Jekyll's relationship with Hyde was most definitely –

Chorus Two – 'Yes but you could see what he was like'

There is a barely hidden violence to this chorus. It is a clear warning to DR STEVENSON *to back off and not ask questions above her rank.* THE GENTLEMEN *start by cutting off* DR STEVENSON *with a snarl in unison –*

THE GENTLEMEN. **Thank you, miss!**

DR STEVENSON (*outraged*). I beg your pardon?

THE GENTLEMEN….**Doctor.**

DR STEVENSON. Thank *you*. Well? What?

THE GENTLEMEN. **Well… look at him.**

JEKYLL *is there for them to refer to – good-looking respectability incarnate.*

Come now, look at him.

A judge of good wine…

A judge of good *character* –

Intelligent –

Affectionate –

And – (*With insinuation.*) **handsome…?**

JEKYLL. Doctor…

Does DR STEVENSON *blush? She does…*

THE GENTLEMEN. **Exactly –**

　　Everybody said so…

　　And… upright.

　　Exactly.

　　Everybody **said so.**

　　*A different rhythm, now – now that they have got her to admit
　　her fascination with this idol of her profession, the threat
　　escalates… perhaps* THE GENTLEMEN *surround her…*

　　Just look at him –

　　D'you see?

　　Very… experienced.

　　Very *senior*.

　　D'you see?

　　Published –

　　Admired –

　　MD –

　　FRS…

　　So, doctor – shall we leave it at that?

　　Shall we?

JEKYLL (*with sinister softness, to* DR STEVENSON).
　　Goodnight.

　　JEKYLL *walks back through the glossy black front door –
　　and closes it behind him.*

　　Mission accomplished, THE GENTLEMEN *turn away from*
　　DR STEVENSON.

　　But…

DR STEVENSON. Excuse me. Gentlemen!

THE GENTLEMEN. **Yes?**

DR STEVENSON. So no one said anything at all?

THE GENTLEMEN. **That's correct.**

DR STEVENSON. And Jekyll himself? What – did he just
    disappear?

THE GENTLEMEN. **Jekyll?**

DR STEVENSON. Go abroad perhaps – for the summer.

THE GENTLEMEN. **Jekyll? – Oh no no no –**

> **Constantly seen around town. Looking a little tired,
> sometimes –**

> **Yes, I noticed that –**

> **But nothing *too* undignified. You know.**

> JEKYLL *now rejoins their number.*

JEKYLL. Thank you.

> *The lights begin to change.* THE GENTLEMEN*'s tone
> taunts* DR STEVENSON *with what they know is coming –
> and what she doesn't. Then, they drop a narrative
> bombshell…*

THE GENTLEMEN. **Until about a year later, that is.**

> *Beat.*

DR STEVENSON. Yes?

THE GENTLEMEN. **Well, practically a year –**

> **October, wasn't it?**

> **Absolutely. October 14th. I was in the club –**

> **Well, we were all in the club –**

> *They all open newspapers and manspread – then, stagily, as
> they all simultaneously spot something shocking in their
> copy of* The Times…

> **Good grief!**

Scene Eleven – Bad News in *The Times*

A gentleman's club.

THE GIRL. What? What was it? 'Ere – did they catch 'im doing something nasty?

THE GENTLEMEN. **Sir Danvers Carew –**

> **Really?**

> **Surely not…**

> **I say…**

> **'MURDER OF SIR DANVERS CAREW – MP'!**

> **Madman suspected –**

> **Singular ferocity of the crime…**

> **High social standing of the victim…**

> ***Shocking* injuries…**

DR STEVENSON (*grabbing her notes*). So this second attack is nearly a whole year after the assault on the girl, but you think it might –

THE GENTLEMEN. **If you say so, doctor. Tell you what – why don't you ask that Mrs Poole for the details. It's *possible* that a housekeeper reads the papers, I suppose…**

MATRON. Bloody cheek.

THE GENTLEMEN. **Thank you!**

Scene Twelve – A Witness Statement, Of Sorts

All the way through this, THE GENTLEMEN *evoke the
killing – possibly a slow-motion echo of its choreography,
possibly something more brutal. For purposes of the plot, their
re-enactment should certainly feature multiple walking canes –
and at least one moment when* THE GENTLEMEN *slam down
their right hands.*

JEKYLL *stays aloof from the action… at least to start with.*

MATRON. Right…

> MATRON *bristles at* THE GENTLEMEN*'s upper-class
> misogynist condescension – then, in defiance of it, becomes*
> MRS POOLE *again. Her text is in counterpoint to their
> slow, sinister action – garrulous, oversharing and even
> salacious as she gets unwittingly caught up in the tabloid
> entertainment value of the atrocity.*

MRS POOLE. Well yes, doctor, it was. Nearly a whole year
later, God bless us. Doesn't time fly? Anyway, there was this
housemaid, apparently – the papers said – and she'd gone to
bed, about eleven o'clock, as you do – and it had been
cloudy, you see, but then there was a moon, you see – and
she was looking out the window, as you do – and suddenly
coming down the lane there was this rather *small* sort of a
young gentleman, the papers said – and he was *approached*,
if you get my meaning, miss, by this other man – who was
an *older* gentleman, you see – white hair, miss, and all very
distinguished-looking… and anyway, they got talking – and
about what, miss, the police never specified, if you know
what I mean – and the next thing, the little one goes quiet all
of a sudden, goes all very impatient and offended-looking –
and he has this cane, see, a sort of a gentleman's fancy
walking cane… and well he sort of *clubs* him. Gets him right
down on the ground, would you believe – hits him so hard he
actually breaks the cane! And then, would you believe it, he
tramples him –

THE GIRL. What?

MRS POOLE. That's right, my girlie. Jumps up and down on
him like he was some sort of a dreadful little ape. Can you
believe it? So she faints – the housemaid – she comes
round – the police gets called, they find the body – all sort of
mangled, it was, blood *everywhere* – and of course they say,
do you recognise him. D'you mean the old one, she says –
and they say yes – and she says sorry no idea, well not with
his face in that condition, officer – and so they say well what
about the other one, what about this little ape-person so-
called, did you recognise *his* face – and oh yes she says, all
of us girls round here know *him*. Never liked him myself. He
gives me the creeps, that Mister Hyde.

THE GENTLEMEN *mark this moment.*

(*Very confidentially – salaciously.*) And apparently, on the
body, there was this sealed and stamped *envelope*. Covered
in blood! The old man must have been on his way to post it,
they said...

DR STEVENSON. Thank you... Yes!

DR STEVENSON *shifts us urgently to...*

Scene Thirteen – Covered in Blood

A hospital morgue.

DR STEVENSON *slips on a white coat covered in blood – and
leads the scene by playing the role of a doctor finishing up an
autopsy. There is a body under a sheet on a gurney (if the
budget will run to that).* MATRON *grabs another coat and
plays her lab assistant.*

UTTERSON *is there – he has been woken up in the middle of
the night and called in to identify the body. Police presence
also –* INSPECTOR NEWCOME, *Scotland Yard.*

DR STEVENSON....the bones of both chest and thorax appear
to have been shattered... there's extensive internal

bleeding... also extensive injuries to the face. It looks as if whoever did this might rather have been enjoying themselves. And this might interest you, inspector. It was found on the body...

She hands the bloodstained envelope to NEWCOME.

NEWCOME (*to* UTTERSON). Thank you, doctor. Any idea, Mister Utterson, why this unfortunate gentleman might be carrying a letter addressed to you personally?

UTTERSON. Because the gentleman in question happens to be Sir Danvers Carew.

NEWCOME (*shocked and impressed*). You don't mean the MP, sir?

UTTERSON. He was a client of mine.

NEWCOME. Really? In which case, this is serious...

The top half of a broken cane is passed to him as a piece of evidence.

Now, this was also found at the scene, sir – snapped clean in half as you can see, but we're doing our best to identify it... don't suppose you recognise it in any way, sir?

UTTERSON *does his best to conceal the fact that he recognises this object.* DR STEVENSON *clocks his reaction.*

UTTERSON. No – but then I can't imagine why you think I should –

DR STEVENSON. Inspector –

NEWCOME. Doctor?

DR STEVENSON. Yes. Did the housemaid give you a description of the assailant?

NEWCOME (*referring to a notebook*). Well, not his face, miss, but... 'Particularly small and wicked-looking' is what she called him. 'Ape-like.'

DR STEVENSON. Then I think Mister Utterson might have something to tell you. Mister Utterson?

UTTERSON. Doctor, you don't understand.

DR STEVENSON. No, I don't, but I fully intend to.

She takes him out of NEWCOME's *earshot for a moment. They speak fast and sotto voce as if to avoid* NEWCOME *hearing.*

You do recognise it, don't you?

UTTERSON (*deeply disturbed*). What?

DR STEVENSON. The cane?

UTTERSON. Yes. (*Making sure* NEWCOME *doesn't hear.*) I once made a present of exactly that cane to my good friend... Doctor Henry Jekyll.

Beat.

DR STEVENSON. What?

UTTERSON. Exactly.

He decides.

Inspector – the creature you're looking for is called Hyde.

NEWCOME. Hyde, sir?

UTTERSON. Mister Edward Hyde.

THE GENTLEMEN *begin to whistle Hyde's tune. It continues, in broken phrases, under...*

DR STEVENSON (*using her notes to check the address*). And he lives in Soho – (*To* UTTERSON.) That's right, isn't it?

UTTERSON. Yes. God help us.

DR STEVENSON. Indeed.

THE GIRL, *a step ahead, gives a piercing two-fingered whistle.*

Thank you. 14 Meard Street please, cabbie – fast as you like!

Chorus Three – The Cab Journey to Soho

In sinister voices, THE GENTLEMEN *sing* HYDE's *nasty little music-hall song. The song is intercut with comments to the audience by* UTTERSON *and* DR STEVENSON *about what they see as they look out of the cab windows – the sex workers of Soho.*

THE GENTLEMEN.
Maybe it's because I'm a Londoner –

DR STEVENSON. The journey was dreadful.

THE GENTLEMEN.
That I love London so.

UTTERSON. Blast this fog…

THE GENTLEMEN.
Maybe it's because I'm a Londoner –

DR STEVENSON. The streets all dismal –

THE GENTLEMEN.
That I think of her, wherever I go.

DR STEVENSON *and* UTTERSON. Women, in doorways –

THE GENTLEMEN.
I gets this funny feeling inside of me –

DR STEVENSON. And children.

THE GENTLEMEN.
Just walking up and down –

DR STEVENSON. *Children*, for God's sake!

THE GIRL (*'You didn't know children worked as prostitutes?'*).
Right…

THE GENTLEMEN.
Maybe it's because I'm a Londoner…

DR STEVENSON *and* UTTERSON. This city's a nightmare.

THE GENTLEMEN.
   ...that I love London town!

DR STEVENSON *and* UTTERSON. A nightmare...

Scene Fourteen – Meard Street

Hyde's rooms in Soho.

DR STEVENSON *and* NEWCOME *arrive in Meard Street.*

NEWCOME. This seems to be the address, sir. Shabby or what?

DR STEVENSON. Not quite where you'd expect to find a man who's heir to a quarter of a million sterling...

UTTERSON. No.

NEWCOME. No, miss – and this woman 'ere says she's Mister Hyde's landlady – (*Looking round to see who's going to fill this vacancy.*) Er – this woman here –

THE GIRL *steps in to play Hyde's* LANDLADY.

LANDLADY. Yes, inspector, Mister 'yde's landlady, good evening – but... looks like Mister 'yde's not at 'ome.

DR STEVENSON. Damn. Sorry, inspector.

NEWCOME. What about last night, ma'am?

THE LANDLADY. Well... last night... I couldn't rightly say...

UTTERSON. This is most important –

DR STEVENSON. Perhaps if you search his rooms –

THE LANDLADY. Oh, I'm not sure Mister 'yde'd like that – but if he's in trouble...

NEWCOME (*giving her money*). Just open the rooms, would you, madam?

LANDLADY. Do come in, inspector.

They search the room.

What's 'e done, eh? Nobody likes 'im, you know. 'E 'urts people... Tramples them. Bastard.

MATRON. Language!

THE GIRL. Oh 'scuse me –

DR STEVENSON. Look at this, inspector – somebody's been burning a chequebook – Coutts bank.

UTTERSON. Let me see –

NEWCOME. And what's that, sir, sticking out behind the door?

THE GIRL. Oh my God –

UTTERSON. Oh dear God. Is that –

NEWCOME *holds the second half of the broken cane very gingerly.*

NEWCOME. I'm afraid it is, sir. So the housemaid was right...

DR STEVENSON. Inspector?

NEWCOME (*trying to shield the evidently queasy* UTTERSON *from the grim details*). White hairs, miss, mixed in with bits of... well, you can see. Would you –

DR STEVENSON *takes care of the evidence.*

Now don't you worry, Mister Utterson, sir. With that cane, I reckon we've got 'im in our sights. We'll get some 'andbills out with a description straight away... get the papers working up a drawing –

UTTERSON *unconsciously wipes his hands on his pocket handkerchief* – THE GENTLEMEN *mockingly echo his gesture.*

Chorus Four – Face of a Murderer

THE GENTLEMEN *as distant* NEWSBOYS – *taunting*
UTTERSON – *maybe with a whistling underscore…*

THE GENTLEMEN-NEWSBOYS. **Read all about it!**

THE GIRL. 'Ang on.

THE GENTLEMEN-NEWSBOYS. **Face of the murderer!**

THE GIRL. 'E still hasn't got no face…

The whistling comes to a taunting halt –

NEWCOME (*back amongst* THE GENTLEMEN). Now I'm
sure I know my job, young lady…

THE GIRL. I mean, not one you could do a description from,
miss. You see it was always –

THE GENTLEMEN. **Yes?**

THE GIRL. I don't know, all right?

THE GENTLEMEN. **Really…**

UTTERSON. She's right. Nobody ever could describe his
face – not even I, and I –

THE GENTLEMEN (*snarling*). **Yes?!**

THE GIRL. 'Ang on… why don't you ask that Mrs Poole, sir –

THE GENTLEMEN *hiss in alarm…*

She knows him from the 'ouse. She'll talk you up a picture –

UTTERSON. Yes! Clever girl.

THE GIRL (*to* MATRON). See? Not just pretty.

Taking charge – but in fact deeply flustered – UTTERSON
wheels the front door out. MATRON *grabs a bit of costume
and hastily becomes* MRS POOLE *again –*

UTTERSON. Thank you. Right, okay – (*Knocks on door.*)
Poole?

MATRON *is just finishing up with her costume, then…*

MRS POOLE. Just coming, sir! Right.

UTTERSON. Good evening, Poole –

MRS POOLE. Sir?

UTTERSON. Look, Poole – no – hang on –

He changes his mind, and decides to go straight to the horse's mouth instead of messing around with this servant.

I tell you what: is Doctor Jekyll in this time?

MRS POOLE. Sir?

UTTERSON. The doctor, woman. Now!

MRS POOLE (*to* DR STEVENSON). Well, I did what I was told, miss – of course I did – took him across the yard, and straight up to the doctor's laboratory out the back there – old place it is, needs a good clean if you ask me – and so there we were, both standing right outside the laboratory door. Weren't we, sir? The *laboratory* door?

Of course, it isn't the laboratory door they are standing outside, it is still the shiny black front door.

UTTERSON. Right… Right you are, Poole.

UTTERSON, *not knowing what else to do, spins the door. This time – the audience not having noticed when this switch was made – what is on the other side of the cabinet is not the shabby back door but the red baize door to Jekyll's study. Standing in front of it, both of them are hesitant. She because she knows something bad is up in her house, he because he now has to confront Jekyll.*

Ominous sound.

Ah yes.

MRS POOLE. Doctors don't like to be disturbed, do they, sir, when they're working.

UTTERSON *seems paralysed.*

I'll do it for you, shall I, sir?

MRS POOLE *steps in, and knocks for him.*

Doctor Jekyll? Doctor Jekyll?

Pause. Noise!

Out through the door steps… JEKYLL. His voice and body have both changed. He seems ill – or perhaps deranged. Perhaps a dressing gown… and he has a bandaged right hand (from beating Sir Carew to death, which we will eventually discover is what he was doing last night). UTTERSON and MRS POOLE are both dismayed by his ashen appearance.

JEKYLL. Thank you, Mrs Poole, if I might –

MRS POOLE. Certainly, sir…

She gets him a chair, and possibly a drink.

JEKYLL. That will be all.

MRS POOLE. I'm sure, sir.

MRS POOLE bobs and exits – i.e. steps out of character and undoes her apron. MATRON – like DR STEVENSON – is dismayed by the sight of someone so obviously in need of medical care.

JEKYLL (*to* UTTERSON). Lock the door.

THE GENTLEMEN-NEWSBOYS (*a sinister whisper*). **Face… of a murderer…**

Scene Fifteen – In Extremis

Jekyll's study.

Note: although the three women are right there, JEKYLL *plays that no one else is in this scene except* UTTERSON.

JEKYLL. I hear the newsboys from my dining room.

UTTERSON. So you know?

JEKYLL. Oh yes.

UTTERSON. Very well then. The police have found the murder weapon. Harry, you have not been mad enough...

THE GENTLEMEN-NEWSBOYS (*sotto voce*). **Read all about it...**

UTTERSON. I mean you wouldn't...

Beat.

DR STEVENSON. Ask him, Mister Utterson, just ask him!

UTTERSON *lowers his voice, so that no one can hear them through the door.*

UTTERSON. You have not been mad enough to hide this monster in your house?

JEKYLL. Utterson, I swear to God – to *God* – I will never set eyes on Hyde again. I'm quite done with him, you see. Indeed, Hyde doesn't want my help any more. You of course don't know him as I do – but trust me, he's safe – quite safe. I promise you, you'll never hear of Mister Hyde again.

UTTERSON. You seem pretty sure of him. If this murder ever comes to trial –

JEKYLL. In fact... I've just received a letter from him. I'm not sure I shouldn't show it to the police – but I thought perhaps I might leave that decision in your hands, Utterson. You're such a wise judge of things. And – of course – I trust you...

JEKYLL *holds out the letter for* UTTERSON *to take.*

UTTERSON. You fear, I suppose, that a letter might lead to his detection.

JEKYLL. Well, I was thinking more of my *own* character... of all our characters, really. Which this hateful business could perhaps rather expose.

Beat.

UTTERSON. May I read it?

The letter is handed over. UTTERSON *reads it.* JEKYLL *watches him closely while making sure that* UTTERSON *isn't aware of him doing this.*

THE GENTLEMEN-NEWSBOYS. **Read all about it...**

JEKYLL. You see... he thanks me for my past assistance – financially... but assures me I need labour under no alarm – henceforth – because he's found himself a sure means of escape. An *absolutely* sure means. And look how he signs off: 'your unworthy servant', et cetera – 'unworthy', you see, he admits that now – 'Edward... Hyde'.

DR STEVENSON (*suggesting a question to* UTTERSON). Ask him if there was an envelope.

JEKYLL (*as if* UTTERSON *had asked*). I burnt it, I'm afraid. But there was no postmark – the letter came by hand.

UTTERSON. I see.

JEKYLL *passes the letter to* UTTERSON.

I'll keep this locked in my safe, if I may.

DR STEVENSON *takes the letter and inspects it.*

JEKYLL. Oh, of course. You decide on what happens next – really I've lost confidence in myself entirely.

UTTERSON (*preparing to go*). He made you put that clause into your will, didn't he?

JEKYLL. Oh yes.

UTTERSON. Hyde meant to murder you, Harry. You've had a lucky escape.

JEKYLL. I've had a lesson. Oh, such a lesson... such a lesson...

> JEKYLL *seems on the point of collapse.*

UTTERSON. I'll see myself out.

> UTTERSON *exits – but not using the locked study door, he just retreats out of the scene.*

JEKYLL (*alone*). Such a lesson...

> JEKYLL *seems to be sobbing – distraught – with his hands over his face... but during the next scene the sobs turn into barely stifled laughter.*

THE GENTLEMEN (*admiringly*). **Such a lesson, doctor...**

Scene Sixteen – 'I don't understand...'

Out in the hall, UTTERSON *is listening to the sobbing, as if he was hearing it indistinctly through the study door.*

DR STEVENSON. Poole?

MRS POOLE. Yes, miss?

DR STEVENSON. That letter – what did the messenger who brought it to the house look like?

MRS POOLE. Oh, nothing's come today by hand, miss – only post, miss. Circulars.

DR STEVENSON. I see...

UTTERSON. Listen!

> *The sobbing has changed to laughter. It stops...* THE GENTLEMEN *whistle a bar of Hyde's song...*

JEKYLL. Quiet!

MRS POOLE. Sir?

> UTTERSON *looks at the letter, deep in thought...*

UTTERSON. I don't understand…

JEKYLL. No, you don't.

> *He rejoins* THE GENTLEMEN. *Perhaps one of them can't resist bursting into giggles like a schoolboy at how well the deception of the last scene worked… Suddenly, one of them offers himself up as someone who might be able to help –* MR GUEST.

GUEST. Never mind, eh, sir – and excuse me for barging in, sir, but might *I* be able to help?

Scene Seventeen – Graphology

Utterson's office.

GUEST *is a junior clerk. His chattiness has an odd way of making things sound obscene. The scene is a kind of music-hall turn – but remember that* JEKYLL *is visible all through this, watching closely from amongst* THE GENTLEMEN, *alert to any possible threat…*

DR STEVENSON. Sorry, but you are?

GUEST. Mister Guest, miss.

> *They shake hands.*

I works as one of Mister Utterson's clerks, and I have this – well, I have this hobby, miss. *Graphology.*

MATRON. I beg your pardon?

GUEST. How you does your handwriting.

THE GIRL. Oh…

UTTERSON. Guest – good to see you. Do come in… So you think you might be able to help?

GUEST. Oh I think I might be able to *lend a hand*, sir – Now…

> GUEST *sets up a blackboard for his demonstration.*

GUEST. – and can I just say, sir, that was a very sad business about your friend the MP, sir. Whoever done that, sir – well, it don't bear thinking about.

UTTERSON. Thank you.

GUEST. Anyway, if I might see the letter, sir – I thank you. A murderer's autograph – not something you see *every* day, boys and girls... ah, 'ere we go. Let's just get that right up there... so to speak...

He chalks up a word from the letter on the blackboard: 'EDWARD'.

THE GENTLEMEN. **Aaaah!**

GUEST. Now, as you can see, it's an *odd* hand – but I shouldn't say myself *mad*.

UTTERSON. No?

GUEST. And now... might you have a specimen of the *doctor's* hand concealed anywhere about your person, sir?

UTTERSON. You mean Doctor Jekyll's?

GUEST. I certainly do, sir.

UTTERSON. Well –

Another GENTLEMAN impersonates an OFFICE BOY – he plays as if he was the stooge in a double-act with GUEST

OFFICE BOY. Excuse me, sir, post for Mister Utterson, sir. Well, blow me down if it ain't a note from Doctor Jekyll, sir!

GUEST. I say, I say, I say – And might that note be anything *private*, young man?

OFFICE BOY. Oh no, sir, it's merely an hinvitation – to dinner, next week.

GUEST. Well, blow me down –

OFFICE BOY. Glad to be of service, sir... (*Sliding out of role.*) So to speak...

He exits the scene, rejoining THE GENTLEMEN.

GUEST. Now let me see...

GUEST *begins to chalk up another word, copying it from the dinner invitation. It reads: 'HENRY'. JEKYLL is visibly alert.*

D'you see, boys and girls – and Mister Utterson, sir. Lots of what we graphologists call in the business *identicalities* – check out that 'E', boys and girls, check out his 'R's... only... d'you see? – the two hands are differently sloped. D'you see – this one dresses to the left – so to speak – that one, to the right. But otherwise, you see... well the two of them might really be... twins.

THE GENTLEMEN-HYDES (*in Hyde's trademark hissing recoil*). **Ah!**

UTTERSON. Yes, I do see, Guest – but I don't want you to speak of this to anyone. D'you understand?

GUEST. Oh, completely, sir.

UTTERSON. Thank you, Guest.

GUEST. Thank you, sir. Ladies...

He rejoins THE GENTLEMEN.

During the following scene, something begins to happen: JEKYLL *calmly puts on a white coat... is this the beginning of the transformation scene that we've all been waiting for? Beakers, powders, maybe even dry ice. The celebration of a kind of blasphemous, white-coated mass with* JEKYLL *as priest, and his* GENTLEMEN *as assistants. An ominous atmosphere builds as if something terrible is about to happen...*

DR STEVENSON (*to* UTTERSON). So I take it that after that conversation you went straight back to the inspector?

THE GENTLEMEN (*wickedly*). **Well...**

DR STEVENSON. In God's name, why not? You now had clear evidence that your client – a senior and well-respected doctor, I might add – had forged an alibi for a murderer!

UTTERSON *puts the letters away.*

Did you not feel any guilt about maintaining that alibi?

THE GENTLEMEN. **Well...**

UTTERSON. Not unduly.

THE GIRL (*hopping mad*). I don't believe people like you!

UTTERSON. Then pay attention to the story! Look, there were plenty of rumours coming out about Hyde's past – his reputation, his violence... but of his present whereabouts – not a whisper. It was as if he had never existed. I mean – didn't you read the papers?

THE GENTLEMEN (*mocking*). **'Suspect leaves no trace...'**

THE GIRL. No, I didn't.

MATRON *moves to protect her.*

THE GENTLEMEN. **Oh?**

'Police abandon hunt...'

THE GIRL. And I can't – all right? I can't *read*.

MATRON. It's all right, my love...

UTTERSON. Well, if you had, then you might have seen this: 'Doctor Jekyll, the noted medical philanthropist, was seen yesterday back at the Royal Society.'

THE GIRL (*fighting back*). What's that got to bloody do with anything?

THE GENTLEMEN. **Oh, Doctor Jekyll was seen at all the best houses....**

UTTERSON. You see?

THE GENTLEMEN. **At a charity concert for the Pacific Missionary Fund...**

At *church*...

THE GIRL. What d'they mean, church?

MATRON. It's all right, dear.

THE GENTLEMEN. **'Almighty God...'**

UTTERSON. They mean, time passed –

THE GENTLEMEN. **'...to whom all hearts...'**

UTTERSON. And Harry Jekyll was back –

THE GENTLEMEN. **'...are open...'**

UTTERSON. He was quite himself again –

THE GENTLEMEN. **'...and from whom no secrets are hid...'**

UTTERSON. And the influence of Mister Hyde was over. Over. Case closed!

THE GENTLEMEN. **Amen.**

THE GIRL (*losing it*). No. You mean – you don't care?!

> THE GENTLEMEN, *in unison, begin to sing a quiet, pious Victorian hymn, 'When I Survey the Wondrous Cross'. Their singing is salacious – weird – unsettling – and continues under the following dialogue...*

THE GENTLEMEN.
When I survey the wond'rous Cross
On which the Prince of Glory dy'd,
My richest Gain I count but Loss,
And pour Contempt on all my Pride.

Were the whole Realm of Nature mine,
That were a Present far too small;
Love so amazing, so divine,
Demands my Soul, my Life, my All...

> *Meanwhile,* JEKYLL *continues his experiment.* MATRON *is comforting* THE GIRL – *but is not at all inclined to let* UTTERSON *off the hook.*

MATRON. Well, you may be right, Mister Utterson – you gentlemen usually are – but what about the other stories?

UTTERSON. Madam?

MATRON. The ones Mrs Poole would have read in her employer's copies of *The Times*. Sir. For instance...

(*In* POOLE's *voice*.) 'Doctor Jekyll's charity concert, intended to take place this afternoon, has unfortunately been cancelled' – (*Her own voice again*.) well, goodness me, sir – and then, the next week, people said she got instructions there were to be no callers. Poole, he said, that door stays shut. Why was that, eh? What was he hiding, in there?!

Her voice is strong enough to disrupt THE GENTLEMEN. *The hymn stops in mid-phrase.*

JEKYLL *calls down, as if through his study door, telling her to keep the noise down.*

JEKYLL. Thank you, Mrs Poole… that will be all. Gentlemen…

JEKYLL continues with his experiment. THE GENTLEMEN resume their singing – but very very quietly, like naughty schoolboys…

MATRON (*fierce whisper, so* JEKYLL *won't hear*). Why was that, Mister Utterson? He even told her to turn you away.

UTTERSON (*defending himself in an equally furious whisper*). I didn't know, all right? I *didn't know*!

The singing stops. THE GENTLEMEN *and* JEKYLL *suspend. Beat.*

DR STEVENSON (*unimpressed*). And what did you do about that? About this 'not knowing' of yours?

Beat.

UTTERSON. I sought advice from another gentleman.

DR STEVENSON. Don't tell me. Another old schoolfriend?

UTTERSON. Watch. Lanyon!

Snap-change of atmosphere. JEKYLL *and* THE GENTLEMEN *all watch closely and anxiously as –*

Scene Eighteen – 'Accursed'

LANYON *comes out of the chorus to assume his role. He has visibly changed... he is terminally ill – may even need help to get into the scene. As he does so –*

UTTERSON. Well, he'd known Harry as long as I had – but then, when I got there – well, I tried to explain why I'd come, but –

LANYON. No. I will not hear that man's name in my house.

UTTERSON. My dear Lanyon –

LANYON. If you need questions answered, sir, address them to him.

UTTERSON. But he won't see me –

LANYON. I am not surprised.

Beat.

UTTERSON. For God's sake, Lanyon, what has happened between you two?

LANYON. I have heard what I have heard, sir, seen what I have seen. Now listen, Utterson – I have only weeks left – (*Preventing him from interrupting.*) I am a doctor, sir, and think I know my own case! When I am gone – and when that accursed creature is gone too – read this. Is that clear, sir, only when we're both of us gone? Goodnight!

He throws down a sealed package of papers and exits. UTTERSON *stares at it. They all do.*

THE GENTLEMEN. **Almighty God, to whom all hearts are open, and from whom no desires are hid, cleanse the inspiration of our hearts. Cleanse them. Cleanse.**

UTTERSON *stares at the papers.*

UTTERSON. Dear Christ in heaven.

DR STEVENSON (*watching* LANYON *go*). What on earth had Jekyll done to him? He looks as if he's dying...

UTTERSON (*calling after him*). Lanyon? Lanyon!

DR STEVENSON. I mean – he must have told *someone* what was happening –

LANYON *has gone.*

JEKYLL *restarts his experiment. He speaks as if in* UTTERSON*'s mind.*

JEKYLL. Utterson, forgive my not seeing you. I have brought on myself a danger that I cannot name – but believe me, dear friend, if I am the chief of sinners, I am the chief of sufferers also. You can do but one thing now... and that is to respect my silence... D'you understand me? Respect it! Yours sincerely, Henry Jekyll.

UTTERSON. That's all there was. Silence...

THE GENTLEMEN *are still. There is indeed silence.*

But...

DR STEVENSON. But what?

UTTERSON. Funny thing – curiosity. Should one mortify it...

DR STEVENSON *and* UTTERSON. – or should one satisfy it?

Their eyes meet. THE GENTLEMEN *all stand.* JEKYLL *picks up a beaker like a communion chalice, and raises it.*

JEKYLL. Amen...

THE GENTLEMEN (*simultaneously, whispering*). **Amen...**

JEKYLL *drinks. He puts the beaker down. No one moves. Nothing happens.*

THE GENTLEMEN *all close their eyes, and seem to brace themselves...*

MATRON *senses what is coming. She grabs Mrs Poole's apron again.* UTTERSON, *also sensing danger, moves to protect* THE GIRL.

MRS POOLE. Oh God forgive us. God forgive us all.

THE GIRL. What? What is it?

UTTERSON. I'm sure it'll be all right –

MRS POOLE. Something very wrong is happening up there…

Something starts to happen to JEKYLL – his head tips back, and his mouth opens…

A strange noise begins. DR STEVENSON takes notes.

THE GENTLEMEN. **Joy.**

MRS POOLE. Oh Lord.

THE GIRL. What is it?

THE GENTLEMEN. **Life. Blood.**

THE GIRL. You're frightening me… (*Starts to wail.*)

UTTERSON. Ssh – ssh –

THE GENTLEMEN. **Life.**

MRS POOLE. God forgive us.

THE GENTLEMEN. **Joy.**

DR STEVENSON. What did you hear, Mrs Poole? Had Doctor Jekyll been taken ill? Please take your time, but I do need to know –

THE GENTLEMEN. **Ah! Nooooooooow!**

The noise has developed. JEKYLL and THE GENTLEMEN begin to emit a monstrous howl of orgasm. Amidst the smash of breaking glass, all the lights go out. THE GIRL screams.

MRS POOLE. Oh bless us God. Bless us God. Bless us God.

DR STEVENSON is the first one to get her torch lit. The next scene is played out in flickering, crossing torch-beams – while a light grows on the isolated and silhouetted figure of JEKYLL, still in his white coat.

Scene Nineteen – The Last Night

Jekyll's house, outside the laboratory door.

In that blackout, three of THE GENTLEMEN *have become* TERRIFIED SERVANTS. *They are armed with pokers or whatever else they have been able to find. All the text in this scene should be overlapping – fast, messy, real.*

UTTERSON. Is everybody here all right?

SERVANT. Thank the Lord you're 'ere, sir.

SERVANT. It's like a beast in there, sir – a beast!

UTTERSON. Quiet, all of you! I'm sure your master would not be at all pleased to see his staff behaving in this manner. Now what *exactly* is it that you're all so afraid of?

SERVANT. The footsteps, sir.

DR STEVENSON. Footsteps?

SERVANT. In there. They ain't the master's.

UTTERSON. Oh come now –

SERVANT. And why's he praying, eh? Why's he praying?

DR STEVENSON. When did you last see your employer, Mrs Poole?

SERVANT. That was eight days ago, miss –

UTTERSON. Let her speak!

MRS POOLE. Last week it was, miss –

DR STEVENSON. And since then?

MRS POOLE. All we've seen is the papers.

UTTERSON. What kind of papers?

SERVANT. Slipped out under the door they are, asking us to go and check in every flippin' chemist in London, sir – and always looking for the same damned thing.

DR STEVENSON *has taken one of the papers and is looking at it.*

MRS POOLE. They're all signed, miss – see?

DR STEVENSON. He's looking for chemicals – some sort of basic salt compound, I think – and look at the writing –

UTTERSON *reads – and sees what* DR STEVENSON *has just seen: that the notes are in Jekyll's handwriting.*

UTTERSON. Jekyll...

SERVANT. I tell you, sir, those noises it's making –

UTTERSON. Thank you. Now, I am sure this can all be explained and made natural –

MRS POOLE. But I saw his face!

This stops things.

THE GIRL. When?

DR STEVENSON. Mrs Poole?

MRS POOLE. Yesterday. I took his tray up, and the door was left open – and I tell you, that's not the doctor. I mean, why would he have a mask on his face? He's been killed, I tell you, somebody's been and gone and killed the doctor!

THE GIRL. Oh my God...

UTTERSON. Hold your tongue, woman – if he's writing notes, he's still alive! Take her to kitchen, somebody, would you –

THE GIRL. I'll do it.

UTTERSON. Thank you. Right, gentlemen: is this door safely locked?

SERVANT. Yes, sir, the master always bolts it from inside.

UTTERSON. Good. And have you an axe in the house?

SERVANT. Sir?

UTTERSON. Go and get it, please. Right –

DR STEVENSON. What about the back door?

UTTERSON. Good point. You two, go round the back. Whoever it is in there, we don't want them escaping that way.

SERVANTS. Sir.

The axe is passed forward to UTTERSON.

UTTERSON. Right.

He calls through the door.

Jekyll, if you're in there, we demand to see you.

Harry? Harry, it's Utterson.

Look, whoever you are in there, I demand to see the doctor. I give you fair warning.

THE GENTLEMEN-HYDES. **Oh, for God's sake, give me peace...**

MRS POOLE (*freaking out*). That's not his voice – that's not his voice.

UTTERSON (*with the axe*). No it's not – it's Hyde's. Stand back please! Harry – hold on – hold on!

The light has been growing on the white-coated figure of JEKYLL. *We see him climb down to the back of the red baize door and then – immediately – without there having been time for any costume change – out through door walks* HYDE. *People drop back as if there was forcefield round him.*

He walks unsteadily to a chair – hops up on it like a monstrous little ape, baring his teeth – but then corrects himself and sits himself neatly upright.

HYDE. Maybe it's because –

Or –

Maybe it's because –

When you think of it –

Whatever you do –

Maybe it's because –

Because… I just love –

But then again –

Oops!

HYDE *begins to giggle, and to shake, and then to bleed from the mouth. He suffers a series of odd little convulsions – and dies, grinning. A small bottle falls from his hand and rolls across the floor.*

THE GIRL *goes to pick it up.*

DR STEVENSON. Don't touch it!

THE GIRL. What?

DR STEVENSON. That smell, is cyanide.

MATRON. Oh, God forgive him.

THE GIRL *rolls the body over with her foot.*

THE GIRL. So that's what 'e looks like.

EVERYONE (*not* DR STEVENSON; *sotto*). **Mister. Edward. Hyde.**

Maybe the lights come back on. Maybe not. But if they do, we see UTTERSON, MATRON, DR STEVENSON, THE GIRL, *Hyde's dead body – but no* GENTLEMEN.

Scene Twenty – Bewilderment

DR STEVENSON. I don't understand. If that's Hyde, where's the doctor?

UTTERSON. Excuse me?

DR STEVENSON. The servants said there'd been notes from Doctor Jekyll all that week, notes which – as you saw – the good doctor had clearly signed himself. Both doors were locked, so where was he?

Again: did nobody call in the inspector?

Beat.

UTTERSON. No.

Beat.

DR STEVENSON. Why in *heaven's* name not, Mister Utterson?

A decision.

UTTERSON. Because I found this – sitting on Jekyll's desk. It was addressed to me, but…

He throws down a sealed document.

If you really want to know what had happened to your precious 'doctor', miss, I suggest you read it. Every single word.

Goodnight.

He exits.

DR STEVENSON (*calling after him*). What else does one do with a mystery, Mister Utterson, but investigate it?

The three women are left alone with the body.

THE GIRL. That's what your job's all about, really.

DR STEVENSON. Sorry?

THE GIRL. Whadjamecallit. Mystery.

DR STEVENSON. Yes, I suppose it is. Matron, could you –

MATRON. Certainly, doctor.

> MATRON *covers the body with a sheet. At least one gloved hand remains visible. She collects Hyde's hat, and puts that on top of the sheet. She removes the cyanide to a safe place.*

DR STEVENSON. Right. (*To* THE GIRL, *referring to all the various papers.*) I think we should start by sorting these into some sort of order.

> *With* THE GIRL*'s help, she starts to sort all the papers – the notes she has been taking, all the documents. She opens the last document* UTTERSON *left behind.*

No...

> THE GIRL *and* MATRON *look over her shoulder.* THE GIRL *looks at the audience.*

THE GIRL. 'Ere! Nosey parkers...

> *All three women look at the audience.*

ALL THREE. Thank you.

> *Light falls on the sheeted body – and that gloved hand. Ominous sound.*

> *Sudden blackout. Darkness.*

> *End of Act One.*

ACT TWO

Scene Twenty-One – Unfinished Business

Lights up abruptly. The three women are all there, as is Hyde's body. It is now on a hospital gurney, still with that distinctively gloved hand poking out from under the sheet, and with Hyde's hat still just where MATRON *put it.*

The papers left by Jekyll have clearly all been read and sorted into piles.

MATRON *is active, tidying up. Mopping disinfectant across the place where Hyde bled as he died, perhaps.*

The lecture-theatre seats are empty – THE GENTLEMEN *are not onstage.*

Seeing that the audience is watching them, THE GIRL *returns their stare:*

THE GIRL. I know – you're thinking, it was no good her staring at all them papers, she can't bloody read. Well – (*Proudly.*) the *doctor*'s told me all about it. The full *bloody* story.

MATRON. That's right – it was all there. Plain as your face.

DR STEVENSON. Everything explained and made natural...

DR STEVENSON *starts packing away the papers.*

THE GIRL. Y'know, what I don't get is: why?

DR STEVENSON. Sorry?

THE GIRL. I mean yes you've sorted all the when and where and whatever, but I didn't hear nuffink in what you told me about no reasons.

DR STEVENSON. You mean –

THE GIRL. I means... that first night, when he ran over me, why didn't he stop?

Beat.

I means, why is it men always 'as to hurt people?

MATRON. Come now, child –

THE GIRL. Don't you 'child' me, missus, I'm arskin' a question.

MATRON. I'm sure the doctor –

THE GIRL. I need to know.

Beat.

DR STEVENSON. Why on earth would you want to go back over what happened to you?

THE GIRL. Let me see... how does it go? Oh yes – (*Mimicking her.*) 'What else does do one do with a whadjamecallit.' You know –

DR STEVENSON. A mystery –

THE GIRL. That's the one!

Well?

Beat.

DR STEVENSON. All right –

MATRON. Surely the dead are best left in peace, doctor.

DR STEVENSON. In this case, possibly not.

What do you say, doctor?

Doctor?

Ominous noise – something moves – the sheet is pulled back from the gurney.

It isn't Hyde.

It sits up – JEKYLL.

Scene Twenty-Two – 'Doctor Jekyll, I presume?'

THE GIRL. What? How'd you do that?

DR STEVENSON. Bodies never lie. In fact, they can't.

JEKYLL. Might I –

> JEKYLL *needs a glass of water.* MATRON *passes him one. He is a wrecked, high-functioning, morning-after addict – and with a throat sore from screaming as he died. It will take a while before his blood starts fully flowing, and before his voice (and mind) come fully back under his control.*

Thank you so much, dear.

I…

> JEKYLL *pulls off the glove that he wore when he was Hyde, and discards Hyde's hat.*

Doctor Henry Jekyll, MD, Fellow of the Royal Society, would like to start –

DR STEVENSON. Doctor.

JEKYLL. Yes?

DR STEVENSON. Did you hear the question?

JEKYLL. Oh yes – the young lady's quite right. One should always go back to the beginning. The basics.

DR STEVENSON. Well then.

JEKYLL. Well then.

Ladies and gentlemen.

Doctor. In the beginning… I, was born rich.

Beat.

DR STEVENSON. Don't stop.

JEKYLL. No.

And as a young man – therefore – I had every likelihood of an honourable and distinguished future. The worst of my faults... as a young man... was a certain shall we say impatient gaiety of disposition. This was a hard thing to reconcile with my aspirations towards our noble profession. Doctor. Other young men might have been free to blazon their irregularities – their more sordid pleasures – but I was not.

So... Doctor Jekyll became double. He lived two lives.

I would argue that this was in no sense hypocrisy –

DR STEVENSON. Really?

JEKYLL. Really. I was equally 'myself' when I laid aside restraint and plunged into shame as when I was at work. Labouring daily – 'for the benefit of the sick, by all and any means required.' You remember, doctor.

DR STEVENSON. I do. And then?

JEKYLL. Ah, then... Gentlemen!

THE GENTLEMEN *re-enter. They brings medical/scientific equipment with them and begin to set it up – white coats, beakers, drugs – as if they were* JEKYLL's *lab assistants.*

Welcome back, gentlemen, do carry on, I'm just explaining the background.

...If only these two 'persons' of mine, I began to think, might be *truly* split. Physically... disassociated. If the 'sordid' or violent part of me – for instance – might walk his downward path delivered from all remorse, while his more upright twin might carry on doing all the good things he was doing, but no longer threatened by Disgrace. Or Penitence. Such a discovery would take science far beyond the mere furtherance of knowledge, I thought – far beyond the simple relief of sorrow and suffering – it would tend, you might say, towards the mystic.

Imagine...

THE GENTLEMEN (*an addict's anticipation of pleasure*).
Aaaah... imagine...

JEKYLL. Well, I did more. At my laboratory table, I learnt to pluck back these merely fleshly vestments, to free... the twins. The fortress of identity *shook* –

DR STEVENSON. How did you do it, doctor?

JEKYLL. Sorry?

DR STEVENSON. What was in the mixture?

JEKYLL. Ah. Shall we just say, doctor, that whatever it was, it worked. As it happens, the powdered form of the *main* ingredient can be purchased from any respectable firm of chemists...

THE GIRL (*interrupting*). 'Ow did it feel?

JEKYLL. I beg your pardon.

MATRON. She said, 'How did it feel?'

THE GIRL. Yeah, like did it 'urt. The first time.

JEKYLL. ...Oh, the first time was incredible. It was... so very sweet.

THE GIRL. Show us then. Go on. I dare you.

JEKYLL. Do you really...?

DR STEVENSON *and* MATRON. Yes. We do.

JEKYLL *laughs... and lets his colleagues know that they are about to give a demonstration.*

JEKYLL. Well. Gentlemen...

Scene Twenty-Three – Transformation

JEKYLL *lectures.* THE GENTLEMEN *each subject themselves to the experiment.*

JEKYLL. First, I waited until after dark. I was worried of course that I might overdose – but the temptation was too strong. I mixed the elements: first the basic salt, then the, er – (*Stops himself giving away the secret.*) tincture. I watched them boil, cool, then drank off the potion. The first symptom was pain. Oh, the most racking pain!

THE GENTLEMEN *feel it go through their bodies. They change into Hyde as the lecture continues…*

Grinding in the bones – a touch of horror, naturally– and then – something quite new – I felt… (*Lists the final symptoms.*) younger, lighter, happier – I think that's the word – but also a kind of recklessness, a sense of… untouchability.

What do you think was the first thing I did?

THE GIRL. Headed out for a local street corner?

JEKYLL (*salaciously*). No, dear. I looked in my bedroom mirror…

THE GENTLEMEN *sigh. Their joy brings them almost to tears…*

JEKYLL. And there I was. 'Animal' – people said later – 'misbegotten'… 'revolting' – but what *I* saw was…

THE GIRL. Yes?

THE GENTLEMEN. **Myself –**

JEKYLL. Myself –

THE GENTLEMEN (*in Hyde's voice, suddenly*). **Myself!**

JEKYLL. – my other, single, natural self. Pure… evil.

THE GIRL (*unimpressed*). Yeah but did it *really* hurt?

THE GENTLEMEN-HYDES. **Oh!**

JEKYLL. Oh, it felt like being born. Like dying!

THE GENTLEMEN-HYDES. **AH!**

> THE GENTLEMEN-HYDES *shudder – with pleasure, or pain – and then begin slowly to restore to their gentlemen-like selves, during…*

JEKYLL. Naturally, I lingered but a moment at that mirror – for there was a second experiment to be done. Should I be able to return, I wondered – or had I lost my other identity beyond redemption? Must I flee before daylight from a house no longer mine? I prepared the cup… drank… suffered… and came to myself once more.

> THE GENTLEMEN *twitch themselves back into Jekyll-ness.*

JEKYLL. Doctor Henry Jekyll…

> MD.

> FRS.

> Rich –

> Respectable –

> Attractive.

> *He looks at his hands for a moment, as if he can't quite believe how easy it was.*

D'you see?

> THE GENTLEMEN *make a few final gestures of tidying themselves up. They are now the very mirror of the doctor's respectability.* JEKYLL *is now much more invigorated. He taunts* DR STEVENSON *with the calmness of his power. She doesn't rise to the bait – but simmers, as this passage builds towards the confrontation between the two of them that follows…*

And it really was that easy.

I christened myself, told my servants that 'Mister Hyde' was to have full liberty of the house –

> MATRON *becomes* MRS POOLE.

MRS POOLE. Right you are, sir, and is he to have a key?

JEKYLL. He is, Mrs Poole. *He* practised my signature – which no one ever dared query –

ENFIELD (*defensively*). Well, I had no reason to suspect –

JEKYLL. Quite, Mister Enfield –

GUEST. It was an odd hand, but I shouldn't have said *mad* –

JEKYLL. While *I* kept on giving dinner parties –

LANYON. Which I later very much regretted attending.

JEKYLL. Oh, did you, Doctor Lanyon? – I took those foul rooms in Soho –

NEWCOME (*defensively*). In which we later found all the clues we needed –

JEKYLL. But never *me*, inspector – and... I added that clause to my will –

UTTERSON. To which I objected to most strongly –

JEKYLL. – but then drew up anyway.

JEKYLL *now flaunts himself in front of* DR STEVENSON. *A rise in temperature – he becomes a tempter.*

You see – doctor – I didn't *risk* anything. I merely planned. A new life. A *new life* – can you imagine?

DR STEVENSON. Of course I can.

JEKYLL. Really?

DR STEVENSON (*right back at him*). Really, doctor. How do you think I got here?

JEKYLL. By planning?

DR STEVENSON. Yes – but I would have stopped, you see... I'd have stopped as soon as I realised what Hyde actually *was*. What he *did*.

JEKYLL. Oh really, doctor – are you sure? All I had to do each night was to get home, swallow a second dose, and whatever Edward Hyde had been up to after dark passed away like the stain of breath upon a mirror. There is no pleasure, my dear, like the pleasure of complete safety. Even my money was immune…

A long beat of danger, and seduction.

Scene Twenty-Four – The First Accident

THE GIRL. And where was I, when you looked in yer bloody mirror?

DR STEVENSON (*getting herself back together*). Yes. Yes – what about her, doctor?

JEKYLL. Her? Oh you, my dear, were my first mistake, my first… accident – but happily, one quite without consequences.

THE GIRL (*showing her bruises*). Oh yes? So I just imagined them bruises, did I?

JEKYLL (*a suggestion of Hyde's voice*). I was late, dear, and I had to get home to my chemicals. (*Complete contempt.*) I was in a hurry…

The scene now builds to an explosion of physical violence. THE GENTLEMEN *are sneering, cool, taunting* THE GIRL – *extensions of* JEKYLL.

THE GENTLEMEN. **A hurry –**

JEKYLL. And anyway –

THE GENTLEMEN. **What was *she* doing –**

At three o'clock in the morning –

THE GIRL. What?

THE GENTLEMEN. *Running*, **I might add –**

JEKYLL. Yes, what *were* you doing, at that time of night?

THE GIRL. I was working. All right?

THE GENTLEMEN. **Look, we were both coming round the same corner –**

She reached it at the same time as I did.

And so quite naturally –

DR STEVENSON. Really? '*Naturally*'?

JEKYLL. Oh *absolutely* –

THE GENTLEMEN. **I didn't stop.**

Cruelty?

JEKYLL. Oh hardly –

THE GENTLEMEN. **Accidentally?**

JEKYLL. Of course.

The scene explodes. THE GIRL *is furious with* JEKYLL*'s callousness – and physically attacks him.*

THE GIRL. Aaaaargh! You nasty, evil – evil little – evil! Let me bloody go!

For her own safety, THE GIRL *is restrained by* MATRON *and* DR STEVENSON. THE GENTLEMEN *intervene to protect* JEKYLL *– they suddenly seem like his bodyguards. Animal noises – that hissing sound – the threat of violence. However,* DR STEVENSON *is in as much of a rage as* THE GIRL. *As they struggle…*

DR STEVENSON. Did you have no *feelings*?

JEKYLL. None, except that of absolute pleasure.

DR STEVENSON. Pleasure?

THE GENTLEMEN-HYDES. **Pleasure!**

JEKYLL (*a voice like ice and fire*). Pleasure, madam – Pleasure, and Liberty.

DR STEVENSON. Hah!

JEKYLL. Don't you see?! It was always *him* doing the harm – him who was guilty. In the morning, I was unimpaired. And also – may I remind you – a hundred pounds, I think I wrote her mother a cheque for.

MATRON. Oh, as if that made everything all right?!

JEKYLL. But it did, madam! Mister Enfield, tell her.

THE GENTLEMEN, *called on to offer more character testimonials, offerHyde-ish impersonations of their characters. Quickfire:*

ENFIELD. **Oh his was a name of great propriety, madam. Great propriety!**

JEKYLL. And Mister Utterson –

UTTERSON. **A most distinguished member of society.**

JEKYLL. Professor Lanyon –

LANYON. **We were at the same school, actually –**

JEKYLL. You see? I was beyond the reach of fate...

DR STEVENSON. You speak as if everything was being done by someone else.

JEKYLL (*triumphant*). It was! I... I mean he... didn't exist...

Beat.

DR STEVENSON. Until October 14th. It was night of the 14th, wasn't it? Shall I check?

THE GENTLEMEN *bare their teeth, knowing she's got him trapped against that fact.*

JEKYLL *hesitates.*

MATRON (*to* JEKYLL). Go on, doctor, you were saying it was always someone else.

JEKYLL. It *was* – always – but then, eventually, as with all drugs...

DR STEVENSON. Yes, doctor? As with all drugs?

Scene Twenty-Five – The Torturing of Jekyll; Or, Addiction

The attitude of THE GENTLEMEN *shifts. They now start to torture* JEKYLL. *If they twitch – even if they smooth their hair – it is him who feels the pain, and cries out.*

JEYKLL. Ah! You see sometimes, when I'd been out on one of my 'excursions', the next morning, I knew where I was –

THE GENTLEMEN *become mocking versions of Jekyll's staff.*

STAFF. **You was in your bed, sir.**

JEKYLL. Yes, and I'd recognise the curtains – ah! – but I had – ah!

STAFF. **You 'ad the odd sensation, sir…**

JEKYLL. That I wasn't in *my* bed at all –

STAFF. **No?**

JEKYLL. Aaah! No, but in the other place –

STAFF. **Reall–**

JEKYLL. – *his* place. Soho. And sometimes – *Aaah!* – sometimes I'd have to double the dose – aaah! –

JEKYLL *becomes a sweaty, this-man-needs-to-go-into-rehab mess – racked with the pain that they are somehow inflicting on him. He tries to get to the powders that* THE GENTLEMEN *used in their previous demonstration – but either they are all used up, or the beakers are empty, or his hands are shaking too much to scrape them out –*

In order to get back home – ah! – triple it – and I said to myself, I said come now, doctor, if this gets any worse – if this gets any worse you are really going to have to *choose* – you're going to have to choose between your two – aaaaarghhh – between being respected, or reviled – between respected – or loathesome – ah! – and of course it did get worse – so much worse – until – on October 14th – on the night of October the 14th – Ah!

As he screams in pain, THE GENTLEMEN *all produce their walking canes…*

THE GENTLEMEN (*becoming murderous, with great relish*). **Ah!**

Scene Twenty-Six – The Killing of Sir Danvers Carew

THE GENTLEMEN. **There was no one watching – no one to see me –**

And the gentleman stopped to ask me the way, and he was so… *old.*

You see.

So polite –

JEKYLL (*as* HYDE). So *respectable*… And I don't know why, but I just wanted… to kill him. Imagine.

This time, we see JEKYLL *in the centre of this re-enactment of the murder. There is no Sir Danvers – just a choreographed ritual.* JEKYLL-AS-HYDE *and* THE GENTLEMEN *swing their canes with great pleasure. The book says that 'in a transport of glee, I mauled the unresisting body, tasting delight with every blow'. While they do it, they sing Hyde's song, and* JEKYLL-AS-HYDE *has fragments of text cut into the song – all accompanied by the swing of their canes. Think of the moment in the film of* A Clockwork Orange *when Alex and his Droogs batter the tramp to death to the sound of 'Singin' in the Rain' – or of Hannibal Lecter swinging his police baton to the sound of Bach when he bashes the face off the handcuffed cop in* Silence of the Lambs *– think of Fred Astaire, and his cane…*

THE GENTLEMEN.
Maybe it's because…

JEKYLL-AS-HYDE. I was in hell, you see.

THE GENTLEMEN.
That I love hurting so...

JEKYLL-AS-HYDE. My life... was hell.

THE GENTLEMEN.
Maybe it's because –

JEKYLL-AS-HYDE. Yet how strange it was –

THE GENTLEMEN.
That I think of it, wherever I go –

JEKYLL-AS-HYDE. I felt such delight – Oh!

THE GENTLEMEN.
I get this funny feeling inside of me –

JEKYLL-AS-HYDE. Oh yes!

THE GENTLEMEN.
As I walk up and down –

JEKYLL-AS-HYDE. But doesn't ev'ryone –

THE GENTLEMEN.
Oh maybe it's because –

JEKYLL-AS-HYDE. Doesn't ev'ryone –

THE GENTLEMEN.
That I love –

JEKYLL-AS-HYDE. Love their life?!

THE GENTLEMEN. **Life!**

JEKYLL-AS-HYDE. Hell!

THE GENTLEMEN. **Life!**

JEKYLL-AS-HYDE. Hell!

THE GENTLEMEN. **Life!!**

They are exhausted.

Panting.

Scene Twenty-Seven – After the Murder

JEKYLL *is now fully* HYDE. *His body and voice are both now weirdly childish. High on the violence. Very dangerous.*

JEKYLL-AS-HYDE. Oh thank you. Thank you, thank you...

DR STEVENSON (*observing him very closely, taking notes*). Don't stop, doctor...

JEKYLL-AS-HYDE. Oops.

He pantomimes trying to clean up his shirt and face – it would be great if he was now covered in blood.

Bit of a problem. How was I to get home to my drugs... Edward Hyde had been described you see – by that *housekeeper* – and I was being hunted. Oh yes. Hunted. By the police, by bloody *women* – my own bloody servants would have shopped me given half a chance. But they were not. Happily for them. And then... I thought of Doctor Lanyon!

He starts scurrying around and setting up the next scene.

Good old kind old respectable Doctor Lanyon. Somebody bring me a pen.

JEKYLL-AS-HYDE *lets out a terrifying snarl. He bites his nails in fury. An impression of great violence.*

I said, someone bring me a *pen.*

Whoever it is, he snarls at them.

Thank you, dear, now *go.* Oops!

Wickedly, HYDE *impersonates* JEKYLL *as he writes.*

Dear Doctor Lanyon, *you* are one of my oldest friends... now, I am not about to ask you to do anything *illegal* tonight, but I thought you'd like to know that your dear old schoolmate Henry Jekyll's life –

THE GENTLEMEN (*prompting*). **Try 'reason'...**

JEKYLL-AS-HYDE. Oh lovely – your dear old friend's *reason* –

THE GENTLEMEN. **Try 'honour'**...

JEKYLL-AS-HYDE. His honour – even better – is at stake tonight.

JEKYLL-AS-HYDE *laughs and sings as he scribbles. He giggles – chatters like a monkey*...

DR STEVENSON. Now I understand about the handwriting –

JEKYLL-AS-HYDE. Who's a clever girl then... (*Finishing his letter with a flourish.*) MD! FRS! Oh, Doctor Lanyon?! Knock, knock!

He holds out the note, and waits. LANYON *seems old and ill as he joins the scene. It is very late at night.*

LANYON. Yes yes, I'm coming...

JEKYLL-AS-HYDE (*seeing him stagger*). Oops!

DR STEVENSON. Don't tell me you helped him?

LANYON. It was midnight, miss. The note I'd received had made me already suspect that my former colleague might be insane – the victim, possibly, of some fairly advanced cerebral disease – but all he'd asked me to do was to obtain supplies, then answer the door to a messenger. I equipped myself appropriately...

LANYON *has a gun –* THE GENTLEMEN-HYDES *react in mock-terror.*

And let him in. Thank you!

We cut to...

Scene Twenty-Eight – An Old Friendship

JEKYLL-AS-HYDE *seems to be of very great physical strength, but also of great apparent debility of constitution – a kind of delirium. He should speak very gently, like some sort of demon child – very high – fast – full of joy.* THE GENTLEMEN-HYDES *should back him up and speak with him as his backing track, as if he was multiple…* LANYON *must keep the gun trained on him at all times.* MATRON *and* DR STEVENSON *must keep* THE GIRL *well clear. They know that the gun is real, and that this creature is dangerous.*

JEKYLL-AS-HYDE. Oh, Doctor Lanyon, how good of you to let me in, there's policemen absolutely everywhere…

LANYON. Its voice, as you can hear, was disgusting.

JEKYLL. Oh disgusting –

LANYON. It was vile.

JEKYLL. Absolutely, and have you got it?

LANYON. Got what?

JEKYLL. Why, the stuff that dear goody-good Jekyll wrote and asked you to fetch from his laboratory for me.

LANYON. If you mean the chemicals that a close friend and fellow professional begged me to fetch here under cover of darkness – take them.

LANYON *throws what might well look like a pack of cocaine.* JEKYLL *catches it – and nearly comes with joy and relief. The other* GENTLEMEN-HYDES *join him.*

THE GENTLEMEN-HYDES. **Oh thank you thank you thank you, Doctor Lanyon, dear friend…**

JEKYLL-AS-HYDE. And might we trouble you for a graduated glass, doctor…

Using an empty glass, JEKYLL *does his preparations – pantomiming the mixing – watching the glass bubble and boil – leaving the potion to cool – until he stands ready with the glass.* THE GENTLEMEN-HYDES *amplify the sequence. They are greedy – animal, mad, childish…*

THE GENTLEMEN-HYDES (*ad lib*). **Oh! Mixy-mixy mix-mix…**

Bubble bubble bubble…

Cool cool cool…

Sippy sippy sip sip!

JEKYLL-AS-HYDE *speaks to* LANYON, *but also to* DR STEVENSON, *even if he is not looking at her.*

JEKYLL-AS-HYDE. And now, doctor… do you want to watch it happen? Do think before you answer – choose aright, and new provinces of knowledge shall be laid open before you: new avenues of power.

LANYON. Sir, you speak enigmas.

JEKYLL-AS-HYDE. Do I? Behold. Oops!

Mimicking a priest at communion, he drinks.

Amen.

THE GENTLEMEN-HYDES *do a step-by-step parody of the traditional business of clutching, staggering – and of being restored to gentlemanliness.*

THE GENTLEMEN. **Our doctor…**

Which art in heaven.

Forgive us our trespasses.

For ever and ever.

Ah –

Ah, men.

During this, JEKYLL-AS-HYDE *also – very simply, with weird self-control – starts to transform his posture and voice back into that of an impeccable – if slightly pale and shaky – JEKYLL. During this…*

LANYON (*to* DR STEVENSON). You see, miss? I *saw it happen* – my God –

JEKYLL-AS-HYDE. God, doctor?

LANYON. In front of my very eyes!

JEKYLL-AS-HYDE. What else should one do with a mystery, but examine it?

> JEKYLL-AS-HYDE *laughs.* LANYON *staggers and clutches at his heart.* THE GENTLEMEN, *acting as valets, help their master to smarten up – we see* JEKYLL *becoming fully his dinner-party self again. Although still bloody, perhaps.*

(*To his staff.*) Thank you, gentlemen, that will be all.

(*Calmly, to* LANYON.) And then, dear Hastie – before I went home – I told you everything.

LANYON. Dear God…

JEKYLL-AS-HYDE. That's right. Carew was murdered by someone who looks exactly… like… us.

LANYON. Oh, God help us.

JEKYLL-AS-HYDE. Oh, if I thought he could do that, Doctor Lanyon, I would never rise from my knees again…

> LANYON, *enraged beyond endurance, puts the gun to* JEKYLL's *head and cocks the trigger.* JEKYLL *cowers and screams –* THE GIRL *and the* GENTLEMEN-HYDES *also.*

DR STEVENSON (*as if she wants him to do it*). Yes? Yes!

LANYON (*gun still at* JEKYLL's *head*). And in that moment, I remembered –

DR STEVENSON. What, for God's sake?!

LANYON. That I took the oath as well. To tread with care, in all matters of life and death. To not play God.

(*To* JEKYLL, *with the ferocity of the dying.*) Rest assured, sir: I took your secret to my grave.

> *He removes the gun from* JEKYLL's *head.*

Thank you!

Scene Twenty-Nine – The Penitence of Doctor Jekyll

THE GENTLEMEN (*a sigh of relief*). **Ah!!**

> THE GENTLEMEN *retreat.* LANYON *staggers back to his seat.*

DR STEVENSON (*despite how shaken she is*). What did you do?

JEKYLL. I went home. I found Hyde's key, and broke it. I told myself…

DR STEVENSON. Yes?

JEKYLL. Never again. Never again would I uncage that person. Henceforth, my name would be Jekyll, and my body, my castle. My refuge.

DR STEVENSON. Did it work?

JEKYLL. I changed! I laboured night after night – for the furtherance of knowledge – for the relief of sorrow and suffering!

> THE GENTLEMEN *are stony – they mimic some small gesture of* JEKYLL's, *thus reminding us that he still has them to contend with inside of himself…*

DR STEVENSON (*sceptical*). For how long?

JEKYLL. Months – I mean, I knew what would happen if the police found my secret! I kept that thought before me, at my desk – in church – in the hospital… And I almost succeeded. Really. Almost succeeded in silencing the voice inside me…

> THE GENTLEMEN *whistle Hyde's song, in fragments, under…*

THE GIRL. But?

JEKYLL. As you say…

> There comes an end to all things. The most capacious measure is filled at last.

> When I fell, it seemed almost natural.

It started to happen while I was out in public, you see.

JEKYLL *feels Hyde stirring. He looks at his hands.*

Oh no…

MATRON (*to* THE GIRL). Come out the way, dear… Now.

JEKYLL. No – no no no…

He shakes his head – doesn't want to go through the pain of another transformation… but DR STEVENSON *needs him to. She gets close, and starts to take care of him – not because she suddenly feels sorry for him, but because she wants the full story. She mops his brow – gives him water – pills – holds him – gets a chair – whatever it takes –*

DR STEVENSON. It's all right, Doctor Jekyll. Doctor Jekyll! It's all right. You can tell me –

JEKYLL *is too exhausted to fight any more. He begins the last scene.*

Scene Thirty – Preparations for a Suicide

JEKYLL. Can I? Thank you, doctor…

DR STEVENSON *has her notebook.*

DR STEVENSON. Of course. And where were you, when this happened?

JEKYLL. St James's Park.

DR STEVENSON. Yes.

She is keeping the patient talking so he won't slip out of consciousness.

Come on, doctor. What was the weather like, for instance?

JEKYLL. Rather fine. I was just telling myself how like other people I had managed to become – actually, how much better

I was than most people. More actively good, you see.
(*Pathetically.*) D'you think that's what brought it on?

DR STEVENSON. So the last attack wasn't unexpected –

JEKYLL. Not really –

DR STEVENSON. Go on.

JEKYLL. There were the usual preliminary tremors – a touch of
nausea –

THE GENTLEMEN-HYDES *begin to stir – one of them
retches.*

That familiar slight sensation of faintness – and then a sort of
heat...

THE GENTLEMEN-HYDES *strengthen.*

I got back inside as quickly as I could...

THE GENTLEMEN-HYDES. **Did you remember to lock the
door, doctor?**

JEKYLL. Of course I did!

THE GENTLEMEN *start to change themselves into the
servants, just as they did at the end of Act One – except that
now them rolling up their shirtsleeves looks like a
preparation for murder...*

THE GENTLEMEN-SERVANTS. **The master always locks
the door.**

JEKYLL. And that felt better – safer.

THE GENTLEMEN-HYDES. **Really...**

JEKYLL. Aaah!

DR STEVENSON. I assume you tried doubling the dosage
again?

JEKYLL. Yes but the pains came back almost immediately. Oh
God!

DR STEVENSON. And?

JEKYLL. I started taking it every six hours.

THE GENTLEMEN-HYDES. **And?**

JEKYLL. You know! Soon, there was only one dose left!

THE GENTLEMEN-HYDES. **Really?**

JEKYLL. I sent out to all the chemists – Aaaah! –

THE GENTLEMEN-SERVANTS. **To every flippin' chemist in London!**

DR STEVENSON. Yes, I see –

THE GENTLEMEN-SERVANTS *tear the letters.*

JEKYLL. But no one had the right stuff – it had to be pure, you see – pure. I tried not to fall asleep –

DR STEVENSON *is now caught between wanting this man to finally damn himself by confessing to her in private… and by her feelings for him as a suffering body. This should be a strange and troubling scene.*

THE GENTLEMEN-SERVANTS. **Really, sir? Why's that then?**

JEKYLL. Because I knew I'd wake up as him!

DR STEVENSON. Sssh – it's all right – I'm here – (*Ad lib – she gets more pills or water.*)

THE GENTLEMEN-SERVANTS. **Imagine…!**

They become more and more animal…

JEKYLL. …but all men sleep, doctor. All men dream… and dear God, the pictures! The cries and voices! The slime of the pit!

THE GENTLEMEN-HYDES *stretch like tigers and crack their knuckles.*

THE GENTLEMEN-HYDES. **Aaaahyesssss!!**

JEKYLL. I equipped myself with the cyanide –

THE GENTLEMEN-HYDES. **Oh, did you now?**

JEKYLL. – because that animal…

THE GENTLEMEN-HYDES. **Yes?**

JEKYLL. – that animal was boiling with hate. I felt him
coming. Coming!

THE GENTLEMEN *go up a gear – they begin to sing their
hymn.*

THE GENTLEMEN-SERVANTS. And why's he praying in
there, eh? Why's he praying?

MATRON (*worried this might all be going too far and that the
patient is in danger*). Doctor!

DR STEVENSON. Doctor Jekyll, do you want to stop now?
If you think we should –

JEKYLL. No! I felt him closer than a wife.

THE GENTLEMEN-HYDES. **Wife!**

JEKYLL. Closer, than an eye.

THE GENTLEMEN-HYDES. **Eye!**

JEKYLL. Caged in my flesh and raging for my blood – and
yet…

He looks at the cyanide – opens it –

Oh, doctor –

DR STEVENSON. Yes?

THE GENTLEMEN-HYDES. **Oh!**

JEKYLL. Oh how he cried – how he struggled to be born! Such
a love of life – such a love of *life* –

DR STEVENSON. No, wait –

JEKYLL. I took the last of my powders, wrote my last words –

DR STEVENSON. No!

MATRON. Let him do it!

JEKYLL. And then –

While I was still – aah!

(*With a supreme effort.*) While I was Doctor Jekyll yet –

I swore –

By all that is sacred in heaven –

*To try and hold on to his sanity in this moment of terror,
JEKYLL recites the doctor's credo with which the show
started. As he recites, we hear HYDE gradually taking
over – the two of them fusing... THE GENTLEMEN mutter
and echo... this is very much an ensemble sequence... an
apotheosis.*

...that I would gladly share all such knowledge as I have
acquired with those who follow after...

THE GENTLEMEN-HYDES. **Pity me.**

JEKYLL. All of it!

THE GENTLEMEN-HYDES. **Have pity...**

JEKYLL. That I have applied all and any measures required –

DR STEVENSON. I know –

JEKYLL. And that I have done no harm.

THE GENTLEMEN-HYDES. **Harm.**

JEKYLL. That I will not be ashamed –

THE GENTLEMEN-HYDES. **Ashamed.**

JEKYLL. That I *will* be respected –

THE GENTLEMEN-HYDES. **Respected.**

JEKYLL. That I shall experience joy –

THE GENTLEMEN-HYDES. **Joy.**

JEKYLL. And healing.

THE GENTLEMEN-HYDES. **Joy...**

JEKYLL. Healing!

THE GENTLEMEN-HYDES. **Blood.**

JEKYLL. Life…

THE GENTLEMEN-HYDES. **Now!**

JEKYLL. Ah no! Not yet. Not yet. Oh! Aaaaaaah!

The last cry is the sound of the two of them. It is one of great release and freedom, as well as one of hate and agony. It is the same orgasmic cry as we heard from behind the door at the end of Act One.

JEKYLL's dead body is exactly where it was at the end of Act One.

MATRON. Oh bless us God. Bless us God.

Silence.

Scene Thirty-One – Aftermath

DR STEVENSON *checks for a pulse.*

THE GIRL. Is 'e really gone, doctor?

DR STEVENSON. Yes. I think he really has gone this time.

THE GIRL. I reckon he was brave, really. You know, doing what he done, to stop hisself.

DR STEVENSON. Everyone has to find their courage.

THE GIRL. You mean like in the very last moment?

Beat.

MATRON. She means in every single moment.

Long beat.

DR STEVENSON. Yes, I rather imagine I do. Thank you, Matron.

Now, shall we get this place cleaned up a bit?

DR STEVENSON *has a long drink of water. The women work.*

THE GENTLEMEN (*softly, to the audience, in unison*). **Thank you...**

Lights out.

The End.

A Timeline of the Story

As mentioned in the introduction I have condensed the timeline of the original novel. Here is the timeline of this version:

The young Dr Jekyll does not consider himself a hypocrite, but he does lead two quite separate lives. His private life is that of a man with the tastes of his class in sex and stimulants, his public life is that of a distinguished doctor, a wealthy philanthropist and a member of society.

In middle age, in the course of some private medical experiments, Dr Jekyll makes a momentous discovery.

He is now able to lead his double life without either shame or fear, because he now has two separate bodies.

To facilitate this double life, he makes a new will, sets up an establishment in Soho, gives his alter-ego Edward Hyde a chequebook and a back-door key (so that he can get back into Jekyll's own house and have free access to the necessary drugs to turn back into the doctor at the end of each 'episode').

Late December: The girl, the first accidental challenge to the double life. Hyde gets away by writing a cheque, which he signs using an impeccable forgery of Jekyll's handwriting.

Hyde worsens – the extended period of the double life. Utterson develops suspicions about Mister Hyde and his relationship with Jekyll. Jekyll has trouble deflecting his concerns – and also those of another senior medical figure, Dr Lanyon – but he manages to keep them both at arm's length.

The drugs and transformations get harder to manage. There is some blurring of the two identities – but it all works. Nearly a year passes...

October 14th: The murder of Danvers Carew. Hyde is identified as the suspect. The police trace him to Soho, but he has already left that address.

The night after the murder: On the run, Hyde tricks Lanyon into getting him the drugs that enable him to turn back into Jekyll.

November/December: After vowing never to take the drugs again, Dr Jekyll devotes himself to good works. Hyde seems to have disappeared entirely, and the police abandon the hunt for Carew's murderer. Jekyll is tempted by the pleasures of life as Mr Hyde, but manages to stay on the straight and narrow.

February: The involuntary return of Hyde – in St James's Park.

Jekyll shuts himself away. He writes to Utterson asking to be left alone while he tries to sort out his problems.

The last week: Jekyll ups his dosage, but the drugs fail. Hyde becomes ascendant.

The drugs run out.

The last night: Hyde threatens to return and take over for good. Jekyll – seeking to put an end to Hyde – takes cyanide. However, it is as Hyde that he dies.

www.nickhernbooks.co.uk

facebook.com/nickhernbooks

twitter.com/nickhernbooks